CARL B. YONG

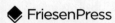 FriesenPress

Suite 300 - 990 Fort St
Victoria, BC, V8V 3K2
Canada

www.friesenpress.com

Copyright © 2019 by Carl B. Yong
First Edition — 2019

All rights reserved.

Disclaimer: While the author made an effort to be factually correct, this is a personal memoir that makes no claim to being an authoritative historical or political work.

No part of this publication may be reproduced in any form, or by any means, electronic or mechanical, including photocopying, recording, or any information browsing, storage, or retrieval system, without permission in writing from FriesenPress.

ISBN
978-1-5255-5321-9 (Hardcover)
978-1-5255-5322-6 (Paperback)
978-1-5255-5323-3 (eBook)

1. TRANSPORTATION

Distributed to the trade by The Ingram Book Company

Dear Cleo and Simon,

This book is for you. I started writing when you asked me how I knew what to do after high school. Now you know the secret sauce.

– Carl Brian Yong

1. THE DRY SEASON

JUNE 16, 1991. It was raining. That was unusual for this time of year on the East African plains. My specific situation was even more unusual, because I was feeling a steady barrage of raindrops inside a tent. *Splat, splat* went the rain, right through the antiquated and worn shelter of paper-thin, vanilla-colored canvas. I was provided with this tired tent by the Taurus Tour Company in Arusha for a four-day safari through Serengeti National Park, Tanzania. We were told that the flimsy tents would be adequate protection from lions, because the beasts would think that the sides of the tent were solid. I was happy to *not* test this assertion. However, these lion-proof tents could not keep out rain.

Our small group of international travelers and Tanzanian guides had enjoyed a second fantastic, blue-sky day of game spotting. We had dinner in the open at a campsite within the national park. The air was pleasantly warm, and there were not many mosquitoes. With no cities nearby to produce light pollution as night fell, we were mesmerized by a star-saturated sky without a speck of cloud. Eventually, at about ten p.m., the chit-chat faltered, and we retreated into our tents. I arranged my things carefully for the night: backpack at my feet, socks tucked into shoes, flashlight next to rolled-up clothes serving as a pillow, and camera and travel papers inside the sleeping bag with me. Now I sat up as droplets of rain landed on my face.

Presently, I concluded that there was nothing I could do about the situation. I resigned myself to a sleepless, damp night and lay back down.

After about five minutes of steady sprinkling, the rain started falling harder. I sat up again in the pitch dark, deciding that I should pack what I could into my water-resistant backpack. It was difficult packing. I crouched on my knees in the confines of the tent, with one hand holding a flashlight. *Thwup!* Suddenly I couldn't see anything at all. The tent had completely collapsed with the weight of the wet fabric. The canvas stuck to my face, and I felt like I was wearing a sheet for a child's ghost costume. Giving up on the now hopeless task of packing, I fumbled about to find the tent opening. I crawled out, just as I heard everyone else's tents collapse. *Thwup! Thwup! Thwup!* Although there was not much wind, the rain had begun to fall in sheets in the worsening storm. Lightning briefly illuminated other campers struggling out of their now shapeless tents.

"Okay. What now?" I said to no one in particular. Only one tent was still standing. A British couple in their mid-thirties had brought their own tent from home for the safari. It was apparently bomb proof, but now it was floating on an inch of rainwater. The grassland had become a shallow lake, and water had started pouring into their tent through its zippered seams from below.

Dumbfounded, all of us stood in the darkness for a few minutes while the rain kept coming down. Our African guides and cooks were sleeping in two Land Rovers parked a short distance away. We were having abortive discussions about cramming into those vehicles to wait out the storm, when abruptly, the rain stopped. There was, of course, no salvaging of a night in the sodden tents. We approached our African hosts to ask them to drive us to the brick and mortar Serena Lodge. The lodge, about twenty minutes away, was one of the few hotels built within the national park boundaries.

Wilfred, our lead guide and game spotter, came out of the vehicle where he'd been sleeping. He gawped at us with wide eyes, stunned. In fourteen years of leading safaris, it had *never* rained like this in the dry season. We were drenched, and by now, shivering. Astonishingly, Wilfred refused to drive us to the hotel. When we pressed, he quietly shook his head. All he could say was, "But who will pay?"

That was the grim reality of life in Wilfred's Tanzania.

"Who will pay?" he repeated. His dazed look was a combination of shock, confusion, and the fear of getting stuck with a bill he could not afford. He suggested that we wait out the night and simply let things dry in the morning sun. It took quite a lot of reassurance that we wealthy tourists would cover the cost of the hotel rooms, and that no amounts would be deducted from the guide's cut of the safari fees we'd paid back at Taurus' office in Arusha.

I thought about the events that had led up to this predicament. I was in the middle of a year-long travelling adventure with a 'round-the-world' airline ticket, and Tanzania was my latest stop. Airlines form partnerships, in which (for a set price) a passenger is permitted to travel around the world once within 365 days, with stops at any of the airports served by the airlines in the partnership. An additional requirement is that the flight segments must be continuously east to west, or continuously west to east, until returning to the airport of origin.

I had bought my round-the-world ticket on a whim after finishing graduate school. After three and a half years of laboratory research, I was thoroughly disillusioned with molecular genetics. I cut short my Ph.D studies. Instead, I defended a Master of Science thesis in front of a panel of university inquisitors. Then I fell into a state of indecision. Faced with the choice of looking for employment doing research, where I had no enthusiasm, applying for more post-secondary education in a different profession, or simply looking for a job, I spent a few aimless weeks in coffee shops and tidying my sock drawer. I told a friend that I didn't know what to do, and she suggested I travel around the world. Perfect. Inside, I thought travel was a great form of procrastination. Outside, I rationalized to everyone who would listen that it was important to see the world, outside of cushy urban Canada, before deciding what to do with my life.

Except for a few trips to some European destinations, I had not travelled much. I had certainly not traveled on my own through developing countries. When Chan, my father, saw my itinerary plans, he was aghast and perplexed. Chan shook his head. "Pakistan? Africa? Why do you want to go there? They're just *poor!*" he exclaimed. He was convinced I would be robbed, lost, cheated, and knifed, not necessarily in that order.

Being a young man in my twenties, I blithely ignored my father's sage advice to stick to wealthy, modern, hygienic nations. Instead, I enthusiastically charted a course for ancient civilizations, underwater worlds, remote places of danger, mystery, human tragedy, the birthplaces of some of the world's major religions, countries with weird and tantalizing foods, thrilling and exotic sports, and jaw-dropping natural wonders. Most of the people on this planet do not inhabit wealthy western democracies. I was determined to see how those people lived their daily lives.

Wet and shivering in the aging Land Rover, we bounced over the soggy grassland as Wilfred drove in the Tanzanian dark. The second vehicle followed with the other half of our group. Somehow, Wilfred found his way easily, even though the headlamps did not illuminate a single landmark I could see in that flat land of so few trees. When we reached the hotel, we joined a crowd of other western tourists who had been similarly caught in the rain. We lined up with our dripping-wet bags as the concierge sorted out rooms for all of us. I watched as Wilfred left us in the hotel lobby, quietly slipping out to spend the night in the car parked outside. Wilfred lived in the world of people without a credit card.

2. BULA!

The man in between waits between the two
Not hearing the lie and not seeing the true.
Unknowing what is and denying what seems
And there he will sleep, the man in between.

"Lady Magdalene"
words and music by Neil Diamond

JANUARY 8, 1991. I didn't think it would be a long way but trudging through sand in thirty-degree Celsius heat and humidity was not fun. After twenty-three hours in airplanes and airport waiting lounges, departing from Calgary, changing planes at Vancouver, several de-icing delays in a snowstorm, and stopping briefly in Hawaii to refuel, I'd landed at Nadi International Airport on Fiji. Now, my sweat-drenched cargo pants and long-sleeve buttoned-front shirt were clinging uncomfortably to my skin. I was lugging a backpack that was heavy with stuff for a year-long journey through countries of radically different climate and terrain. Since I'd left Calgary in the grip of winter, my feet were still encased in heavy leather mountaineering boots.

I sighed, rolled up my sleeves, and kept walking southwest towards Seashell Cove Resort. I told myself I'd soon be rewarded with a relaxing snooze on the beach. I had booked a reservation at the modest two-star hotel. It would be wonderful to get there in a few minutes, peel off the boots, and jump into a pool.

The thought of hitch-hiking had excited me for years. I was envious of stories told by Gordon, a fellow graduate student at McGill University. Gordon was seven years older than me, and as a teenager, he had hitch-hiked across Canada. He cautioned, however, that by 1991 it had become too dangerous to hitch-hike in Canada. However, according to the guidebooks, hitch-hiking was still a safe and common mode of transportation in Fiji. Eager for my first experience thumbing a ride, I walked out of the Nadi airport in sweltering mid-day sunshine, right past the touts and taxi stands. Somehow, I found a kindly Fijian lady in the parking lot, with an open-top jeep, who asked me where I was headed. I gave her the name of the resort. She smiled broadly and offered to give me a lift. *Well, that was easy.* I gladly accepted, and we waited a couple of minutes more for another man she had come to fetch at the airport.

The man who joined us gave the woman a brief hug, and the two of them got into the jeep. The woman would drive. I clambered into the back seat with my pack, and the jeep set off.

The country of Fiji is formed by a group of over three hundred volcanic islands in the Pacific Ocean. We were on the largest island of Viti Levu, which accounts for more than half of the nation's land mass. Viti Levu is also home to Fiji's capital city of Suva. Queen's Road runs along the circumference of circular Viti Levu, and few roads cut through the rugged interior of extinct volcanoes. We headed west along the coast on Queen's Road counter-clockwise from Nadi airport in the south. I stared like a tourist as we drove past mud-colored shrimp-farm ponds, verdant sugarcane fields, wild ponies, cattle, red earth, and mangroves lining the shore. The wind generated by the moving car was refreshing. Then the jeep came to a stop.

My kindly Fijian lady, who had become much less effusive as soon as we'd left the airport, turned to face me. She demanded five Fijian dollars, and told me to get out. No resort in sight. No beach in sight even. She pointed up a dirt road that branched off the asphalt highway.

So much for hitch-hiking and riding on the generosity of strangers. I still wonder why I simply handed her the money, since she hadn't completed her end of the deal. I could have given her the finger and walked away, or at least paid her less. I guess I was just being Canadian. The jeep drove off.

So, there I was, walking along the loose sand shoulder of a dirt road wide enough for motorized vehicles. Although I had walked around at home in the house with my backpack, this was the first time I'd had to hoist it for a fair distance in a foreign land in tropical heat. The pack contained many heavy items I regretted more with every step: a hardcover notebook to serve as a journal, guidebooks for all of the countries on my route (Australia, South East Asia, the Indian subcontinent, Africa, and Europe), binoculars for African safaris, an SLR camera plus 35mm film canisters, aluminum flashlight and pocket knife, heavy-duty mosquito net, tent and propane camping stove for trekking in Nepal, a second camera that was waterproof to fifty feet below sea level, and a big black, wide-brimmed Stetson hat to save me from sunstroke. At least I had decided against lining the pack's interior with chicken wire. The wire was suggested by some travel guides to prevent a stealthy knife from slitting the bottom of the pack behind me while I walked, allowing the perpetrator to grab and dash with anything that fell out.

Thank God I hadn't packed a snorkel mask and fins for my scuba-dive training. That was the plan: spend the first week in Fiji getting a scuba-diving certification, and then use it at other world-class diving locations as I travelled.

I had seen no one else on the road for at least twenty minutes when a pickup truck pulled up beside me. The driver asked where I was headed on this deserted part of the island. He laughed when I told him. He was the manager of the surrounding sugarcane fields, doing his rounds to keep tabs on other employees. I was informed that Sea Shell Cove Resort was ten miles away. The man in the truck gave me a lift most of the way (free of charge), but I still had to walk the last mile to the beach.

Eventually I arrived in the afternoon, super sweaty, parched, and foot sore. The resort had a small hotel with a crowd by the pool. It looked like a giant had thrown a huge sand-flinging tantrum. There were a couple of snapped palm-tree trunks, a collapsed thatch awning, and piles of sand everywhere. I guess I didn't get the memo about the hurricane that had passed through there about a week earlier. Surprisingly, Sea Shell Cove Resort was well attended anyway. I joined a pick-up beach volleyball game along with Germans, Aussies, Kiwis, Yanks, Canucks, and one Spaniard. Other than the Fijian staff, no "people of color" were there, and I was the sole Chinese-Canadian.

I was able to start a four-day PADI (Professional Association of Diving Instructors) diving-certification course the very next day. Joining me were Mariana, a Spanish kindergarten teacher, and Brent, an American restaurateur (a.k.a. waiter). Our instructor, Adrian, also hailed from the United States.

Scuba diving for the first time, using the hotel pool to practice, was exhilarating. At first it felt weirdly unnatural, breathing in from the regulator mouthpiece while your brain screams, *Don't inhale! You're underwater!* After a few minutes, it became easy to review the hand signals, clear a flooded snorkel mask while submerged, and form a habit of regularly checking depth and air gauges. My biggest challenge was maintaining neutral buoyancy. I just couldn't get the knack of constantly adjusting the inflatable scuba vest (a Buoyancy Control Device, or BCD) so that I wouldn't either sink like a stone or need to kick frantically downward to stay at a constant depth.

On the fourth day of the diving course, we headed out on a boat to Namotu Island. The reef near Namotu was the location for our final "open water" diving-certification test. During the entire ride to the island, I worried about my ability to maintain neutral buoyancy.

We three students had arranged ourselves lying down as flat as possible in the motorboat. The small boat had no cabin or cockpit for the driver, just a powerful outboard motor mounted at the stern. It was a brilliant sunny day in the tropics, but the sea spray splashed us with the rhythmic cresting of the waves in the constant wind. Nobody was wearing a wetsuit. I put on my sunglasses and placed my wide black hat on my otherwise bare chest to block the sea spray as much as I could. Nevertheless, my teeth were chattering by the time we got to the dive site. I glanced over at Mariana and Brent. Mariana wore a fetching black maillot swimsuit. Brent wore swimming trunks and had only his chest hairs to block the wind and spray. Mariana and Brent both looked relaxed and comfortable on the ride, while I shivered. My arms ached from tensing to keep from being thrown each time the boat hit a larger wave.

Eventually, the boat slowed and then bobbed gently in the swells at the dive site, with Namotu Island behind us. Adrian gave us our final instructions and a pep talk. Then all four of us plunged under the surface. Descending into the ocean, I breathed in and out too rapidly in my excitement, like most novices, wasting precious scuba-tank air. That first dive was thrilling. I took it all in, looking up to the bottom of the motorboat at the surface, then 360 degrees around me, then below as the colorful alien world of fish and coral engulfed me. Diving in crystal-clear tropical water can give you a false sense of safety because of the high degree of visibility compared to diving in murky water at northern latitudes. You need to remember that you are still ninety feet below the waves. That is a long way to go for a breath if your scuba tank runs empty.

All three of us passed the tests. Afterwards, celebrating back at the Seashell Cove bar, Mariana and Brent talked about how frozen and miserable they had been on the speedboat. Ironically, they had both been amazed at how comfortable and relaxed I'd looked on that ride. Everyone masks their vulnerabilities in public.

After a night of Fiji Bitter beer and goodbyes to Adrian and Brent, I departed with Mariana to explore the island for a few days. I would soon discover that Mariana was more successful than me at flagging down rides. Perhaps because she was better looking? She was a slim brunette with short hair styled in a sassy, wavy bob. She had alluring, dark Latin eyes from her Spanish mother. However, at just over five feet tall, she did not inherit her German father's height. She spoke English with a very slight lisp. Mariana was fearless and loved haggling and markets. For her, this trip to Fiji was a temporary escape from teaching at an elementary school and less-than-exciting work at her father's shoe-store business in Madrid. Here was a woman who loved kids and shoes but needed a walk on the wild side every so often.

We got a lift from staff at the resort to the nearest bus stop, and then rode the bus to the city of Suva on the opposite side of Viti Levu. We then tried to arrange air transport from Suva to the Fijian island of Kadavu to the south. Kadavu is surrounded by the Great Astrolabe Barrier Reef, renowned among scuba divers. Unfortunately, there were no return flights to Kadavu available before our scheduled dates for onward travel from Fiji. We decided to backtrack to Pacific Harbor and go diving at Beqa Lagoon on Viti Levu instead. Mariana was quickly able to flag down a passing motorist. I gratefully hopped in next to her for the free ride.

Pacific Harbor is a small town, reached by a short bridge, on the most southerly part of the island. The town calls itself the "adventure capital of Fiji." It was raining in the adventure capital when we took a chartered boat to the Beqa Lagoon reef, twenty minutes from the shore. However, the grey skies above the waves did nothing to diminish the spectacular scenery below. In our first scuba-diving adventure after being certified, we saw an amazing underwater world of vivid red and blue fan corals, seemingly right out of television documentaries on the Knowledge Network. The lagoon has a dozen dive sites in over 200 miles of coral reef. Beqa lagoon's main attraction for divers is to see sharks up close at specific locations where dive masters have conditioned the sharks to come for feeding. Mariana and I did not see any sharks; they had migrated elsewhere at that time of the year. However, we did see clownfish in the anemones, colorful butterflyfish, surgeonfish, giant groupers, and schools of shiny, intimidating barracudas.

We spent the next two nights in a single-room bungalow on the beach at Tabua Sands. The rental unit consisted of four cardboard-thin walls around a concrete-slab foundation, a thatched roof, and a couple of one-inch-thick sleeping pads. There was not much luxury, but the room came with a matching price tag.

Mariana at the Tabua Sands beach hut in Fiji.

Everywhere we ventured, Mariana made cheerful self-introductions to the locals. While exploring the volcanic rock of the beach, we met a Fijian man collecting coconuts. He invited us back to his home in the tiny village of Namada. Here, we were introduced to *kava*.

Kava is a drink made from the powdered root of the yaqona plant, releasing kavalactones that act as a mild sedative. The drink is commonly described as lukewarm, slightly bitter, muddy water. The grey-brown liquid numbs your lips and tongue and produces a feeling of calm. Fijians invite you to drink kava with them the way we in Canada would offer guests a beer or wine, only kava comes with more ceremony. The kava, prepared in a utilitarian white plastic bucket, was poured into a large earthenware bowl and then served in traditional coconut-shell cups. Our hosts explained the proper way to drink kava. The men must drink first, and then the women. Step one: Clap once and say, *"bula,"* which means "hello" or "love" in the Fijian language. Step two: Drain your cup of kava all in one gulp. Step three: After you swallow, clap three times more.

The kavalactones in the drink soon make everyone relax. You are not afraid of expressing yourself, and everyone begins to talk freely. Often, Fijians sit down to the kava ceremony in order to settle arguments. Even without any special occasion, many Fijians will drink kava daily.

Our Fijian hosts gave us a lesson in the politics of Fiji. They explained that the nation is a democracy, and as in all democracies, population is power. The Fijian islands were peopled with indigenous Fijians, as well as Indians brought over by the British during the colonial period to work in sugarcane fields. By the 1990s, it was a well-established rule for all the Fijians to vote for Fijian political candidates, and for Indians to vote for Indian candidates. On that small Pacific island nation, about half the size of Vancouver Island in Canada, there was little inter-mingling and even less inter-marriage between the two races. In almost every conversation we had with local people on Viti Levu, mutual dislike between Fijians and Indians was palpable.

In between gulps of kava, the Fijians proudly told us how there were separate school systems to ensure that racial prejudices were perpetuated into the next generation. Whether a Fijian government or an Indian government is elected is determined by whether there are more Fijians or Indians to vote. Campaigning politicians encouraged their respective ethnic group to have more babies than the other race.

Leaving Namada, Mariana flagged down an army truck carrying two soldiers. The driver was a chatty Fijian named Joe. The other soldier was a taciturn Indian who scowled at us and only grunted occasionally. They had obviously not volunteered to be in the truck together. We proceeded north to a prawn hatchery near Ba, where we watched the two men unload sacks of prawn feed in the humid sunshine for an hour. It never occurred to me to ask why two soldiers would be delivering prawn feed. Joe had agreed to take us onwards to Nadi after the cargo was unloaded.

Mariana clambered about like a monkey on the mangrove roots lining the shore, while the soldiers were busy. I watched her lithe form from dry land and took pictures, by now quite smitten by this vivacious, confident explorer woman. I was scheduled to catch a flight to Sydney, Australia the next day. Mariana had given me her address in Madrid. She said that she would expect to see me there when I finished my year of travel.

In Nadi, Mariana and I had our last lunch together. It was Mariana's favourite: Chinese food. The Chinese restaurant owners were intensely curious about me. It turned out that their family history and mine were similar. They, too, were part of the Cantonese-speaking diaspora that had fled when the communist tide of Mao Tse Tung surged over China in the 1950s. I asked why the couple had chosen to settle in Fiji, even though they mentioned they had also considered Canada and the United States as destinations. They replied, in a matter-of-fact tone, that North America was too cold.

Education has always been a priority in my family. Perhaps it was because my mother was bitter from being denied her dream of becoming a doctor when she was a teenager. Regardless, both my parents were determined that their children would not be saddled with low-wage labor to earn a living. Mom and Dad believed that education was the key to avoiding that fate. Be educated or be poor.

Today, the only university in the country of Fiji operates in the city of Lautoka. That university would not be open until 2004, more than a decade after my visit to Viti Levu. This Fijian couple running the restaurant had been more concerned about a country's climate than having access to a university. After Mariana and I had finished our meal, the couple told us of their grown children, who were my age and employed in retail. Their son ran a news kiosk at the airport. How easily that might have been me, working at an airport kiosk in Fiji, if my parents had only wanted to be warm. Who knows? I might have been happier living with kava every day.

3. PREHISTORIC BLUE SHRIMP

BEFORE I TRAVELED in Australia, I never knew the island continent could be so wet. I had grown up with mental images of the vast *outback* of a country devoid of lakes and rivers—the treeless, flat, and arid Nullarbor Plain, and sun-drenched beaches extending from Sydney all the way up to Cairns. But here I was, in February, and half of Australia seemed to be underwater. Rains were flooding roads from Adelaide in the south, up every inch of the curving eastern coastline, to Darwin in the north. Only Perth, far away on the west coast, was not drenched. *Can't control the rain*, I thought. *I just have to choose my next move when the clouds roll in.* I would be adjusting my itinerary to dance in and out of clouds over the coming months.

I decided to visit the Kakadu National Park near Darwin. Most people visit the Kakadu to see wildlife and camp under clear skies during the dry season from June to September, but I bought into the tourist advertisements urging adventure-seekers to experience the Kakadu while it is "gorgeous in the wet." Joining a group of other backpackers, I found an incredible guide, Greg, who charged a hundred Australian dollars for a two-and-a-half-day tour of the Kakadu in his minivan. Greg was able to spot some amazing wildlife that had been invisible to the rest of us. He would be driving through the park, then suddenly hit the brakes, jump out and climb a tree, dash into the brush, or slither on his belly to catch something. Without Greg, our tour group would never have noticed the termite mounds, frill-necked lizard, crocodiles, wallabies, or dingoes through the rain-smeared windows of the vehicle. Greg even made us eat honey-drop-flavored ants.

There was water, water everywhere. The unceasing rain was comfortably warm. We parked a short distance away to walk to the aboriginal cave paintings at Nourlangie Rock. We all wore our street clothes, soaked to the skin in the rain, making our way through a flooded paperbark tree forest with mud squishing between our toes, carrying our shoes. Afterwards, we walked over to Broalba Springs for a swim in the rain. But tramping barefoot in flooded muddy forest was, well … just plain soggy. I caught the next bus and headed for dry weather at Alice Springs.

On the bus from Darwin, it appeared that the only people who traveled in Australia were backpackers. I didn't see a single traditional suitcase. Backpacks sporting flag patches of every country except the United States filled the cargo compartments in the belly of the bus. Because of the dim view much of the world had of the US government at the time, any traveling Americans on the bus either had no patches on their luggage or were masquerading with flags of other countries.

Rain obscured the night-time view out the windows along the highway. Several times the bus slowed to a crawl, forcing its way through flooded sections of the road. And then the driver, an unfailingly cheerful fellow, announced over the bus speakers that we were about to try a very Aussie "can do" maneuver.

It was clear that the water on the road immediately ahead was deep enough to submerge the cargo compartments. "If everyone is willing," the driver said, "we're going to empty the cargo bays, and you can each bring your pack up with you to your seat inside. That way, your things will stay dry while I try to drive the bus through this flooded section."

A feeling of team spirit spread amongst the passengers. Besides, the other option was to turn the bus around and head back to the nearest town to find lodgings for the night. No one wanted that. And no one wanted to be seen as a "wanker" (a trendy Australian derogatory term referring to an undesirable person addicted to masturbation). And so, we all enthusiastically trooped off the bus, in the middle of the night-time outback onto the shoulder of the highway. The rain was a drizzle, and there was no other traffic in sight. The driver and some passengers produced flashlights. Hands reached to claim one pack after another, as they were hauled out from underneath the vehicle. Everyone carried his or her pack up into the bus, settling in with packs on laps.

In my imagination, the bus backed up for a running start, just like in a cartoon, before plowing ahead into what looked like a small lake. In reality, we didn't back up to enter the water with momentum. But I wondered how the driver knew the floodwater would not rise high enough to stall the engine. The bus actually did slow but did not stall. Then everyone could feel the gradual rise as we went up the slope on the opposite side. Cheers erupted.

We continued to sit with our packs on our laps for another two hours, plowing through more flooded road sections.

The next morning, I finally escaped the rain as I continued south on another bus. I was entering the colorful and strangely well-organized desert of Australia's interior. The depressing grey-black skies gave way to hundreds of mini-cumulus clouds. The cottony-white clouds were neatly arranged and regularly spaced in a deep blue background. Correspondingly, the vegetation on both sides of the highway changed from dripping rainforest to small, tidy, symmetrical scrub bushes varying in shade from blue-gray to dark green. The bushes were also regularly spaced apart, as if planted by humans in the orange desert soil. We passed a couple of blindingly white salt lakes and unusual flat-topped table mountains.

Backpack travel is a national pastime in Australia. Perhaps because of the country's relative geographical isolation from other wealthy western democracies, Australian youth typically don a pack and travel for months or even years to see the world after finishing school. This is called "going on a walk-about," a phrase that was popularized in the *Crocodile Dundee* comedy movie of 1986. Most Aussie youth eventually return to pursue careers in Australia.

Aussies backpacking around within their own country is just as popular as international travel. In 1991, up to half a dozen backpacker hostels in every major Australian city would send their minivans to greet intercity bus arrivals. Each minivan would be creatively painted and advertise the rate (ten to fifteen Aussie dollars per night) and amenities, such as a pool or coin laundry facilities. Just get off the bus, pick a minivan, and off you go. What could be easier?

Once in the hostel, foreign visitors need to deal with the Aussie accent. As I entered the common lounge area at an Alice Springs hostel, a shirtless, smiling, tanned Caucasian man in his late twenties looked up from a magazine and greeted me.

"Ott dye, might," he said.

"I'm sorry? What was that?" I asked, pausing mid-stride.

"Ott dye, might," he repeated.

I must have looked as baffled as I felt. Mystified, I returned his smile and muttered, "Um, yeah. Thanks." I nodded at the fellow and continued to my room. Hours later, replaying the sounds of his words in my head, I finally managed to puzzle out what he had been saying: "Hot day, mate."

———◇———

I had left Canada in a time of optimism. In 1982, Deng Xiaoping finally allowed Chinese families to sell their crops for personal profit, setting impoverished communist China on the road to becoming the economic juggernaut it is today. In 1985, Mikhail Gorbachev ushered in *perestroika* (restructuring) and *glasnost* (openness) to the Soviet Union, pushing communist Eastern Bloc governments from power over the next five years. In 1986, the World Exposition (Expo) was celebrated in Vancouver, Canada. In 1988, Yasir Arafat promised that the Arabic Palestine Liberation Organization would renounce terrorism and recognize the Jewish state of Israel. In 1989, the Berlin Wall was taken apart, and East and West Germany re-unified after forty-five years of Cold War. In 1990, black political dissident Nelson Mandela was released by his white jailers, marking the beginning of the end of apartheid racial segregation in South Africa.

It was 1991, the beginning of the final decade before a new millennium, and the world was hopeful. For a moment.

In the hostel at Alice Springs, guests were watching television to keep tabs on Operation Desert Shield, also known as the first Gulf War. Iraq had invaded and annexed Kuwait. To free the people of Kuwait from this brutal oppression, the United States had declared war on Iraq. The US formed a multi-country coalition of United Nations countries, including the Arab countries of Saudi Arabia and Egypt. This US-led coalition had invaded Iraq earlier that month to liberate Kuwait.

Everyone in that room full of international backpackers at Alice Springs, including those who admitted to being American, said the White House was using the annexation of Kuwait as an excuse to invade. The true US motives were to protect American oil interests and satisfy a personal vendetta that US President H.W. Bush held against Iraq's president, Saddam Hussein. There had been too many other international atrocities where the US had politely declined to intervene, like the ethnic cleansing of Armenians, or the Cambodian killing fields of the 1970s. The US certainly would not feel the need to save a million Tutsi citizens from genocide in Rwanda in 1994, nor to protect Rohingya people from mass murder in Myanmar in 2017.

None of the backpackers in the room thought the Gulf War would escalate. None believed it would end soon either. Israel, allied with the US, was contemplating nuclear retaliation after Iraq attacked Israel three times with Scud missiles. Iran, which was not a member of the military coalition, feared the massive troop build-up by its neighbour Turkey, which *was* a coalition member, was simply a ruse and that Turkey was in reality preparing to invade Iran. In several countries, especially the Arab allies of the US, Hussein was gaining public sympathy for being unfairly singled out and victimized by the US bully.

In the west, it was a shockingly sanitized war. Journalists were "embedded" in the US military. They broadcast picturesque footage of the daily launch of jets from American aircraft carriers. We were shown banks of US missiles framed by beautiful pink sunsets. Images of Iraqis being blown up, troops in combat, or towns being bombed to smithereens appeared to have been censored. It was a stark contrast to the familiar, horrific black and white images from the two World Wars. Contrary to my expectation that the US would always be an unswerving beacon of transparency and freedom of the press, it seemed America took a Great Leap Backward to restrict journalism and peddle propaganda, just like the communist countries America often criticized.

It was a relief to be dry and free from Darwin's mosquitoes, fleas, and flies.

Alice, as the town is affectionately called, was the starting point for bus tours of Uluru (formerly known by the colonial name of Ayers Rock) and Kata Tjuta (formerly called the Olgas). Both of these giant sandstone monoliths jut upwards with near vertical walls, erupting without warning from the surrounding thousands of square kilometres of flat, flat desert. The high point of Uluru is 348 meters above the plain, while the highest dome in the Kata

Tjuta group is 546 meters above the desert. Uluru and Kata Tjuta were formed deep underground. These homogeneous sandstone blocks then resisted erosion as tectonic forces tilted and pushed them upwards for more than 500 million years. The sandstone blocks reached for the sky, while the softer material surrounding them was eroded away to the featureless desert of today.

The land containing Uluru and Kata Tjuta was confiscated from the indigenous aboriginal population in the early 1900s. Since the 1950s, the land has been operated as a park by the Australian government. With the evolution of society and recognition of indigenous rights, the land was handed back to its aboriginal owners in 1985, under a co-management agreement with Australia Parks. Australian aboriginals continue to live in the area as they have for at least 30,000 years. Uluru and Kata Tjuta have great spiritual significance to these aboriginals; the monoliths are featured in many aboriginal creation stories. The aboriginal owners have always asked that visitors refrain from climbing the monoliths. Their request fell on the deaf ears of western tourists. Since the days of the first European explorers, tourists see Uluru simply as an invitation to climb.

Climbing Uluru was certainly at the top of my mind, and those of my newfound backpacker friends in Alice Springs. My three companions were Michel, a garrulous youth from Holland, and two Irish girls, Cindy and Breda. The Dutch guy was very proud of his packable, crushable hat, which protected him from sun, wind, and rain. I was envious, saddled as I was with my large and rigid black Stetson. Cindy and Breda constantly exchanged funny one-liners in their musical Irish lilt.

Our group of four got up in the middle of the night for the tour bus departing from Alice at 4:30 a.m. The intent was to witness the famous sunrise glow of Uluru. Uluru and Kata Tjuta were about 450 kilometres from town.

After just over four hours of travel, the bus approached Uluru as the night sky was brightening. Fulfilling the promise in the brochures, we stopped and parked some distance away just a few minutes before dawn. Passengers filed off the bus to take photos from that vantage point, where the entirety of Uluru could be seen bathed in the rays of morning. Unfortunately, the sunrise view of the rock was nice but not all that impressive. The backpacker chatter later was that the awe-inspiring events when Uluru looks like a giant glowing rock at sunrise happen only occasionally, when atmospheric conditions are favorable. The bus-tour advertisers neglected to mention that detail.

About a half hour after sunrise, our bus proceeded slowly around Uluru on a packed dirt road. At the time of my visit, the debate still raged on whether the Australian government should pave the road encircling Uluru. Bus wheels were changing the desert. The tires were creating a depressed trough, which affected drainage. In addition, dust churned up by the bus tires was coating the adjacent desert vegetation. Those against building an asphalt road had arguments ranging from aesthetic, fearing an unsightly black band encircling the iconic landmark, to ecological, warning of irreparable damage to natural drainage patterns.

At several points, the bus stopped to allow us to take photographs. Eventually, the passengers were deposited near the head of a trail up the western face that provided the easiest access to Uluru's summit. At the time, there were either no signs asking tourists to not climb Uluru, or we were simply oblivious. There were no aboriginals hanging around to make the request personally. Our group of four proceeded up the rock with all the excitement of youth, completely ignorant of aboriginal sensitivities or disapproval. It would take another twenty-eight years before the Australia National Parks agency agreed with aboriginal owners to ban climbing at Uluru.

Uluru was surprisingly large, but the well-worn path to the summit was easy and gradual. The only steep segment was near the start. A steel chain handrail had been installed on this portion, with the chain suspended at regular intervals by metal rods driven into the rock. With one hand on the chain, it was only slightly more difficult than ascending a steep set of stairs. The rest of the 1.6-kilometre walk, over gentle, smooth parallel mounds to the summit, had no significant vertical climbing. That morning, our group of four followed a steady stream of tourists up the path. At many points, you could see all the way down to the desert, which was quite flat except for the outline of Kata Tjuta behind you in the west.

Tourists going up the path on the left to the peak of Uluru in Australia.

Reaching the summit of Uluru at 863 meters above sea level, we discovered a short, sturdy masonry column about three feet tall installed on the highest mound. The column was octagonal and capped with a matching octagonal brass plaque. Raised print on the cap provided details of Ayers Rock, and arrows pointed in the direction of various cities of the world. There was also a visitor's book for signing. I wondered what would happen to the book when it was filled (and the dozens before it), or if it would be ruined during the rare instances of rain. The past three years had seen unusually high rainfall, explaining the particularly vivid desert vegetation, washed free of road dust.

It was moderately windy at the top with a few wispy clouds. Around the perimeter, you could see the desert plain far below. The surface of the rock at the summit was the same worn, pitted, and striated sandstone as along the entire trail. There were no distinctive features near the summit pedestal other than a small puddle a short distance away. It was an oval depression filled with rainwater. The puddle was about three feet wide, five feet long, and perhaps a foot deep.

The puddle's orange rock bottom under the liquid was clearly visible, with a few pebbles and a bit of sand. Peering into the water, we were astonished to see two alien-looking, blue tadpoles swimming around. The creatures were about an inch long, with shield-shaped heads and two-pronged tails. How did they get into that pond, so high above the desert, and what did they eat? A nearby interpretive sign installed by Australia Parks speculated that the weird blue shrimp were possibly remnants from a previous geological time, when Uluru was part of a wetland. Seeing these living fossils was just as thrilling for me as reaching Uluru's summit.

A quarter of a century later, Uluru shield shrimp had been found across the Australian desert. It turns out that their eggs can survive dormant for years after a pond dries up. Baby shrimp hatch when it eventually rains again. The shield shrimp on Uluru were probably from eggs blown up there recently by desert winds. Sometimes scientific research can completely deflate a terrific mystery.

After returning to Alice, our party of four was stranded in town by flooding on all roads out to the coasts. We retreated to a local bar named Toddy's. Michel regaled us with tales of petty thievery, smoking marijuana, and the disgusting places he had spent the night during his shoe-string budget travels. He described thin mattresses that smelled like sweat and semen, infested with bed bugs. He also provided a litany of travel advice: Townsville sucks, because there is nothing to do there; Adelaide sucks because everything is expensive; Sulawesi in Indonesia rocks with loads of cheap seafood; Phuket in Thailand sucks because it smells like a sewer; Koh Samui rocks with the best warm ocean waves.

Inspired by Michel, I ditched my black Stetson and shopped for a new hat. I found a smooth leather, wide-brimmed hat, made by the famous Australian company Akubra. I loved how I could crush my new hat into a pancake in my backpack. I also found a waxy product to coat the thin light leather for water resistance.

After Michel's stories, I couldn't wait to visit South East Asia.

4. NAZIS IN PENANG

I MADE MY WAY from Australia to Singapore before taking a bus to the city of Jahore Bahru in Malaysia. Singapore was a shockingly regulated city, with an ultra-modern airport guarded by machine-gun-toting doormen, six-lane highways, signs everywhere prohibiting chewing gum and spitting, air-conditioned underground mass transit, uniquely nauseating public washroom stenches, and everywhere poor neighbourhoods being bulldozed to make way for glistening skyscrapers and apartment buildings. Singaporean English-speakers were everywhere. Once I crossed the border to Jahore, however, I was stumped by a language wall.

At home, we often make a big deal about Canada being a multicultural society. Malaysia is also a multicultural country, but with a cultural mix very different from that of Canada. Malaysia is not an established white Anglo-Saxon society absorbing influxes of visible minorities. Instead, Malaysia is a fascinatingly egalitarian blend of three main ethnic groups: Muslim Malays, Taoist Chinese, and Hindu Indians. In Malaysian cities, there was usually nary a head of brown, blond, or reddish hair in sight.

Public government signs in Malaysia are posted in four languages. In addition to the official language of Malay, the signs include Chinese, Tamil (the language in India's state of Tamil Nadu), and English. There are vanishingly few white people in the country, but English is still the language of business and used in schools to teach math and science.

Unfortunately, most restaurants did not have quadrilingual menus. I was puzzling over a menu posted outside a Malaysian diner when I was rescued by Jasmine, an attractive twenty-four-year-old from Singapore. Jasmine had long, straight, jet-black hair cascading down almost to her waist, a ready generous smile, and big brown eyes. She was dressed in a short-sleeved blouse and designer jeans, with stylish black leather pumps on her feet. Jasmine cheerfully translated the menu for me, and then we both went inside. She took a seat across from me when a table became available. We shared a meal of *sambal sotong*: rice with squid, green onions, and a spicy hot sauce.

Jasmine wanted to know all about how she should prepare for travelling. She wanted to see Europe and visit as a solo woman. I assured her that excellent guidebooks were readily available, and she would have no trouble touring most attractions in Europe without harassment. I relayed other lessons I had learned so far. Travel light. Spend more time at fewer destinations. Take money to buy the things that you won't need until later during your journey, if you visit several destinations; you will almost always find those items on location at better prices. Finally, there are invariably good reasons why most tourist attractions are attractions, and why low season is low season.

I'm not sure how much Jasmine was genuinely interested in my travel advice, but I was happy to spend time in her chatty, good-looking company.

I made my way from Johore Bahru to George Town on the island of Penang. This island is connected by a bridge to the west coast of Malaysia and has a colorful history. In the 1700s, Penang was part of the Muslim kingdom of Kedah. Penang was mostly uninhabited until Captain Francis Light of the British East India Company landed his ship there in 1765, using the island as a base to trade in spice and opium. Eventually, the Sultan of Kedah offered Penang to the King of Britain, in exchange for British protection against Siam and Burma invading from the north. In 1786, Britain officially took possession of Penang, renaming it "Prince of Wales Island" and building Fort Cornwallis.

During British rule, many Chinese immigrated to Penang from Fujian Province of mainland China. Today, ethnic Chinese make up about 40 percent of Penang's population. Similarly, ethnic Indians from the province of Tamil Nadu of India came to British colonial Penang as impoverished laborers, seeking to work and send money back to families in their homeland. Since the time of Captain Light, the Penang government has promoted racial and religious tolerance, establishing a stable blend of the three ethnic groups. As a result, the descendants of the Chinese and Tamil migrants have achieved complete social and economic integration with the indigenous Malay population as doctors, lawyers, businessmen, and politicians. The historical core of Penang, George Town, was designated as part of our World Heritage by UNESCO for its unique architecture and Fort Cornwallis. The modern economy of Penang is powered by electronics manufacturing, medical tourism, cruise-ship visits, banking, and jewelry making. The inhabitants of Penang have the highest gross domestic product per capita in the country of Malaysia.

I walked down Pitt Street in George Town and passed a Christian church, Muslim mosque, Hindu temple, and Taoist temple all within meters of each other. I stopped to gawk at the site with the most activity: the Taoist temple of Kuan Yin, Goddess of Mercy (and fortune, and fertility, etc.). Inside, the temple was choked with incense smoke; outside, the air was filled with fluttering ash from two huge metal pot-bellied urns burning ceremonial money. An unending stream of Taoist

Chinese queued to visit, each waving a dozen incense sticks clutched in their hands. The incense was placed before the selected deity figure from whom the visitor wanted to ask a favor. A bell-ringing monk added to the cacophony of voices in prayer. Within the temple courtyard, business was brisk as boxes and boxes of incense and ceremonial paper money were purchased for the unquenchable fires.

Taoism began in China 2,500 years ago with the writings of a man named Lao Tzu (who may or may not have really existed). Lao Tzu wrote about the *Tao*, or "way", as a philosophy that describes the nature of knowledge, reality, and existence. From observing the natural world, Lao Tzu concluded that there exists a natural cosmic harmony, and that a person should follow the Tao to live simply, peacefully with others, and in balance with nature. Then the emperor of the Tang Dynasty was so impressed with Taoism that he decided to declare it to be the official religion of the country.

Taoists do not believe in an omniscient or all-powerful God or gods like those of Christianity or Hinduism. However, over the millenia, Taoists appear to have borrowed gods from other traditional beliefs. Taoists believe that certain humans, including war heroes, emperors, and scholars, have been able to achieve immortality and become gods. Kuan Yin (or Guanyin), for example, was a Chinese woman of kindness dedicated to helping others. Despite mistreatment by the cruel king who was her father, she refused to marry for his political gain unless the king eased the suffering of the poor, old, and sick. Kuan Yin was transformed into a goddess when the king tried to have her executed.

I guess Taoists don't find it odd for the cosmic harmony of the natural world to include a few immortalized humans.

Kuan Yin Temple, Malaysia. Worshippers buy incense and ceremonial paper money from the kiosk on the left. One of the pot-bellied urns, with its opening faced away, is in the centre of the frame.

I left the temple of Kuan Yin and continued towards the food stalls near Fort Cornwallis by the water. Along the way, I spotted young Indian couples holding hands, truant Chinese teenagers in the park, and serious Malaysian businessmen walking briskly with their briefcases to the city hall.

While all the races are integrated into Malaysian society, they are not integrated with each other. Indian politicians took out ads in the newspapers, urging fellow Indians to marry young, marry Indian spouses, and have more babies. In 1991, Indian politicians saw the situation as dire. Over the preceding decade, the ethnic Indian population in Malaysia had fallen from 10 percent to 9 percent of the country's total population. This meant fewer Indian citizens to vote for Indian politicians. To Malaysians, the idea of voting for the best candidate regardless of race was simply absurd and ignorant of how society really works.

The Penang citizens I met who could speak English tended to be well aware of, and connected to, the rest of the world. I had a long conversation with a Chinese businessman in a café. He was relaxed and proclaimed that he was only average, because he was too well-educated to be ruthless in his business dealings. He travelled regularly to Europe. He had two adult daughters, educated in London, England. One daughter was practicing law in Kuala Lumpur, while the other was studying law at Cambridge. That did not sound average to me. In fact, not much about Penang seemed average.

The best thing about Penang was its desserts. Not your typical western desserts of ice cream, gelato, pie, cheesecake, or crème brûlée. Penang dessert was usually a mound of cold beans and syrup. Seriously. On several occasions, I ate this concoction as a lunch substitute in the steamy tropical weather. At the outdoor seating areas, vendors with pushcarts would sell all manner of Malaysian desserts. My favourite was the popular *eis kacang* (pronounced 'ice ka-chang'), a glorious fantasy of sweet corn, gelatin, tapioca, red beans, and ice shavings, piled high in a disposable plastic bowl.

After a few days of exploring George Town and the nearby beaches, it was time to move on. I proceeded to the local shopping centre, where the international bus station was located.

"No seats to Hat Yai tonight. No seats February twenty-first. No seats twenty-second. No seats twenty-third. Twenty-fourth?" suggested the fellow behind the glass in the booth looking at me.

I had just waited twenty-minutes in line to reach the ticket-sales window at the bus station. I wanted to purchase a bus ticket from Malaysia into Hat Yai, Thailand. "You mean, I can't get to Thailand until the twenty-fourth?" I asked.

The ticket seller diligently consulted his computer screens again, pausing for agonizing moments as he scrutinized each prospective date. Two minutes later, he said "No. No seats."

"What about to Butterworth?" I asked. Butterworth was the other Thai city that served as an entry point from Malaysia.

"No. No seats," he answered.

"Are you sure?" I pressed. I could not believe the routes were so popular that every seat on multiple buses each day, to two different Thai cities, were completely sold out for the next four days.

"No. No air-conditioned seats until the twenty-fourth," he confirmed.

"But I don't need an air-conditioned seat," I clarified.

"That's different," he said, and consulted his computer screens a third time. After another two minutes, he said, "Tonight, no seats. No seats twenty-first. Twenty-second, four seats left."

"Terrific," I said, smiling.

"Go down to wicket number fifteen to buy ticket," he advised.

I could see another twenty-minute line-up at wicket number fifteen. "Terrific," I muttered to myself.

After spending another night in George Town, I had a farewell dinner with two other travelers I had befriended, Spike and Martin. Spike was a Malaysian national on vacation from Kuala Lumpur, and he spoke English quite well. Martin was a British *ferengi*. The term "ferengi" would become well-known as a bigheaded, big-eared, misogynistic, and greedy alien race featured in the television series *Star Trek: Deep Space 9*, which would debut in 1993. Years earlier, the term "ferengi" was already commonly applied by Malaysians to Caucasian foreigners.

The three of us wandered George Town in the pleasantly warm evening. We passed an ear-piercing generator, powering an ear-piercing Chinese opera performed on an outdoor stage. Bored kids sat hostage to their octogenarian guardians, filling rows of folding chairs to watch the show. We proceeded past them through the old town streets towards the shore. Away from the generator noise at the quiet along the pier, each wave lit up with the eerie blue-green glow of aquatic micro-organisms. You could see small fish in the shallows, illuminated by the surrounding effervescence. Loitering teenagers threw litter into the water at the fish.

Dinner was ridiculously inexpensive from the food stalls on the wharf. Martin, Spike, and I feasted on *murtabaks* (Indian pizza), Hainan chicken rice, and *nasi goreng ayam*. I requested that last dish when the server came to our table, phonetically reciting, "Nazi Goring I am."

Martin, seizing on the similarity with Nazi officer Hermann Goring, immediately quipped, "But fascist Mussolini you are not." We were howling with laughter all night.

5. PATPONG

I CROSSED THE BORDER by bus into the city of Hat Yai in Thailand. I was oblivious that only three days earlier, on February 23, 1991, the Thai military had taken over from the country's democratically elected government. The crisis resulted when opposing politicians and military generals accused Prime Minister Chatichai Choonhaven of making himself rich while bungling the nation's economy. The coup took place when Mr. Chatichai tried to appoint a renegade sympathetic general as his Minister of Defence. In response, the most powerful generals of the country united. They formed a group that seized power and revoked the constitution.

The Thai generals called themselves the National Peace Keeping Council. They promised to rewrite and improve the constitution, and then hold democratic elections as soon as possible. Prominent politicians were put under house arrest. After this outrageous suspension of democracy at gunpoint, the people in streets of Thailand were filled with ... relief or indifference.

Within days, the country would be treated to a surreal spectacle. Revered Thai King Bhumibol, like a stern father, publicly scolded both the politicians and the generals alike, literally on their knees during a national television broadcast. The king told them to stop fighting each other and start working together for the public good. Without hesitation, the politicians and generals apologized. They pledged to do as their beloved king requested.

It helped that this was the seventeenth successful military coup in over two dozen attempts since 1932, the year Thailand had abandoned rule by absolute monarchy. It also helped that King Bhumibol Adulyadej was a humble man devoted to the welfare of his subjects, and he had been king since 1946. Every Thai person I met loved Bhumibol. Bhumibol would still be king for the military coups to come in 2006 and 2014.

Today, it seems that Thailand still hasn't been able to find the right balance between the competing interests of urban intelligentsia, rural poor, and military power brokers. Thailand's military seems to want both democracy, and also to remain in control. Five years after it seized power in 2014, the military leaders fulfilled their promise and held elections in 2019, but with a new Constitution where one third of the seats in parliament are appointed by the military instead of being elected. The Thai generals appear to want to be certain that the prime minister of their choice is "democratically" elected.

The 1991 coup was almost amusing in its "business as usual" impact. The mega-industry of Thai beach vacations, temple tourism, and sex tourism simply shrugged and moved on. The only difference I noticed was that foreigners were called "ferengi" in Malaysia, but *"farang"* in Thailand.

From Hat Yai at the border, I proceeded to the fairy-tale setting of Thailand's Koh Phi Phi. Beautiful Phi Phi island is roughly shaped like a barbell. A cluster of karst limestone rock outcroppings juts up from the sea on each end, connected by an isthmus with a long sandy beach on both sides. Phi Phi is possibly the world's only double-sided beach, bordered on the north and the south by the warm turquoise of the Andaman Sea. The island air was laced with the scent of ripening fruit from cashew trees. Seeing all the couples on the beach, my thoughts drifted to Mariana. I wrote her a long letter describing events since we had parted.

Scuba diving from Koh Phi Phi was certainly economical. It cost me only fifty Canadian dollars for two dives from a motorboat, with every piece of equipment rented. It was pleasant, although the undersea life did not compare to the reefs at Fiji. Unfortunately, on my second dive, I exceeded the depth tolerance for my underwater camera. I went to fifty-five feet below sea level, five feet of water pressure more than the camera could withstand. The viewfinder glass cracked. The saltwater made quick work of corroding the internal circuitry. Underwater film cameras in the 1990s were much heavier and more expensive than their compact digital counterparts that would arrive twenty years later. I had carried that heavy four-hundred-dollar camera halfway around the globe. After taking fewer than a dozen underwater photographs, the camera was ruined. As Padma would say, "Brilliant."

From the beaches of Phi Phi, I travelled to Bangkok to witness first-hand the traditional Thailand martial art of *Muay Thai*, or Thai kickboxing. Muay Thai is known as the "art of eight limbs" because the boxers can hit each other with eight points of contact (kicks, punches, and blows using knees or elbows), rather than the two (fists) in western-style boxing. I didn't believe real Muay Thai would resemble the spectacular maneuvers portrayed by Jean-Claude Van Damme in Hollywood movies, but I was curious. Would it be as disappointing as watching real-life gambling in Las Vegas casinos, after watching glamourous but fictional Las Vegas gambling in the movies?

Ratchadamnoen Stadium in the Thai capital simmered with a sea of spectators in the cool night air. The two combatants entered the boxing ring wearing shiny silk shorts and traditional headbands. From my distant arena seat, the pair looked well matched, with similar height and build. In fact, I couldn't tell them apart except for the colors of their shorts. Oriental flute music with a slow drumbeat pierced through the murmurs of the crowd. The boxers knelt, bowed their heads towards each other, and prayed for victory.

The centuries-old sport of Muay Thai has been blunted somewhat by the process we call civilization. Now there are rules. Each modern match consists of five timed bouts, and each bout lasts for three minutes. At the first bell, the ever-present music had a regular, measured, and unhurried beat. The boxers tested each other, almost nonchalantly, while the spectators maintained polite interest or placed their final bets. When the bell ushered in the second round, the action picked up. Flying feet, bruising knees, swinging elbows, and pounding fists sent shockwaves into the crowd. In that second round, the boxers were more vicious and more determined. Each solid blow landing was greeted with a loud "Ooph!" from the audience.

The tempo of the flute music increased in each subsequent round, and the fighters corresponded with more frenzied movements. By the fifth round, the sound of the flute had become a crazy jangling. The drumbeat rumbling was almost drowned by the noise of the crowd. Now, neither fighter held anything back. Red-shorts guy seemed to be getting stronger, landing more blows, while the punches from yellow-shorts guy started looking a bit feeble. Still, both men continued to dance, now circling, now attacking, with their lithe, sinewy forms moving quickly around the boxing ring. Even in round five, both combatants still had enough energy to dart their feet high up at their opponent's head, right until the final bell. It was a marked contrast to the lumbering super-heavyweights of western boxing I'd seen on TV. Typically, western boxers appear almost sluggish in the final rounds, sometimes clinging to each other in exhaustion. The Thai boxers, in contrast, were graceful, agile, fast-moving, and they kicked the living shit out of each other.

At length, I'd had enough of Bangkok noise and smog. I would head out to Maenam Beach on the island of Koh Samui the next morning. Although there weren't any drinking buddies around in the hostel, I figured it was *de rigeur* to sample the famous Patpong red-light district before leaving the capital. As a precaution, I took out all but one hundred Thai *baht* from my wallet. I put the balance of my cash into my traveler's money pouch, checked directions in my guidebook, and stepped out for a night of adventure.

Bangkok has many red-light districts, but the others target local Thai men while Patpong aims its entertainment at western farang. Patpong consists of two parallel streets, Patpong 1 and Patpong 2, just west of Lumpini Park. A third parallel street, often called Patpong 3 but officially named Silom Soi 4, provides fleshly delights for gay farang. The Patpong streets appeared seedy and dispirited when I arrived, less than an hour before midnight. There were neither vagrants in the doorways nor beggars reaching out to the farang. Even with brightly lit neon signs, however, the strip-bar facades looked tired and faded. I walked around the two blocks, eyeing potential establishments where I could spend my money.

A tout was stationed outside the door of every bar, urging me to enter. The touts would smile as I passed, calling out, "No pay money, just look five minute!" "One beer, fifty baht!" "Come! Very good show!" "Lots of girls! Lots of pussy!" I picked one of the less flashy places that seemed not too busy and not too empty.

Inside, there were perhaps a dozen worn wooden tables and half that number of patrons watching from scattered seats. A couple of white guys were quietly talking, sipping their drinks in a darkened corner table. On stage, naked Thai girls were doing acrobatics with their genitals and ping pong balls, rolls of toilet paper, and flaming sticks. They danced, twisted, and contorted into provocative poses with their props. The music consisted of Thai versions of western pop melodies. I was ushered to a table off to one side, with an unobstructed view of the stage.

A server arrived promptly and took my order: Singha beer. It was nice to be in an air-conditioned room, a respite from Thailand humidity and mosquitoes. I sipped my drink and watched the show, wondering who dreamed up those crazy acts. One of the serving girls, naked except for a thong bikini bottom, stopped at my table, holding a shot glass full of clear liquid. Probably rum. She smiled, kissed the rim of the glass, and said, "For luck" in English. She did a small bow, tilting her head, and then placed the glass near the edge of my table. I eyed the drink suspiciously but made no move to touch it, continuing to sip my beer from the bottle. Perhaps she would come and retrieve her drink when she finished on stage?

That hope was dashed as a series of topless girls in micro-thongs paraded past my table over the next twenty minutes, each performing the same ritual as the first. Now there were eight shot glasses in a neat row in front of me. I ignored them, finished my beer, and soon had enough of the show. The performers on stage made no pretense of enjoying what they were doing. I stood up, motioning for the bill. Then I noticed that another fresh, cold, opened bottle of beer had materialized next to my elbow when I wasn't looking.

"Just a minute. Just a minute! Can you sit down a minute? I make out the bill for you." The grinning Thai fellow assiduously approached and tugged me by the arm back into my seat.

Okay, I thought. *Seems like an overly formal procedure for a fifty-baht beer, but I can be reasonable.* I sat back down.

"One thousand baht!" he announced. "All these drinks on your table." He showed me a bill listing two beers and eight shots, priced at a hundred baht apiece.

I stared at the bill he was holding up, gaping. Not my sharpest moment, but I finally clued in.

"I ordered a beer," I said, surprised at my own calm. "That should be fifty baht, just like the guy at the door said."

"You owe," the waiter insisted, waving his paper at me, "one thousand baht!"

"I didn't order those other drinks. I'm only paying for the one beer," I countered.

The waiter hesitated. Then, to my relief, he said, "Okay." He bent and wrote up a fresh bill. He handed me the new slip of paper. Then he announced, "Three hundred *baht* for beer. Seven hundred *baht* for sex show. One thousand *baht!*"

I took a moment to digest the new calculation. "Well," I said, "I'm only paying for the one beer I asked for." Starting to stand up, I was caught totally off-guard and off-balance when he pushed me roughly back into the chair. I was a head taller than this fellow and outweighed him by at least fifty pounds. My shock changed to anger. It must have shown on my face, because another employee of the club hurried up to the table and said, "Calm down. You speak to the manager."

I prepared myself for the good cop, bad cop routine. The situation did not look great. Several other Thai men materialized, loosely surrounding my table. I couldn't get over how scrawny they all looked. The bizarre comedy peaked as a topless showgirl, boobs jiggling, also joined the group of thugs. She faced me while holding her arms outstretched, apparently to prevent me from dodging around her to escape.

I looked around the room to see how the other customers were reacting to this commotion, and then realized there were no other customers. The two white farang were gone. The stage was empty and silent. Drapes had been drawn over the windows. Five Thai men and a naked girl now clustered around my table, watching menacingly. The other showgirls stood quietly in a group in the opposite corner, also glaring.

I had no intention of waiting to speak to a manager. I pulled my wallet from my pocket. I fished out the sole one hundred baht note, making certain everyone could see there was no more money in the folds of the wallet. "Look, all I've got is this one hundred baht," I said, as I moved to walk around the little knot of thugs.

The closest one put his hands on my chest and started pushing me back.

Are you kidding? I thought. I was much taller than these skinny guys with bad haircuts. Without thinking, I planted my feet and gave the fellow pushing me a quick two-handed shove up and away. His eyes went wide as his feet left the ground and he sailed backwards. He was saved from the fall by his companions.

"All I brought is one hundred baht," I repeated, glaring defiantly and brandishing the bank note. I spread my wallet open again. "Take a look for yourself. What are you gonna do?" I challenged. I was twenty-eight, had neither a partner nor dependants, and testosterone was sloshing in my veins.

The leader who had written up my bills snatched up the empty wallet. He glanced inside and threw it back on the table. Then he darted forward and frisked me. He pressed on my pockets, feeling for a wad of cash, and then ran his fingers along my waist searching for the bulge of the money belt worn by all farang tourists. I was too surprised at this brazen personal intrusion to do anything before he was finished. No cash, no money belt.

Disgusted, he stared at me with mounting animosity. Then he muttered something in Thai to the others, shaking his head and relenting. Looking disappointed, all the Thais withdrew as their leader pocketed my hundred-baht bill.

I took my cue and walked out, not hopeful that I would get any change for the fifty-baht beer. Once outside on the street, I checked over my shoulder periodically, in case they followed me for an ambush. The streets were deserted, although you could still hear crowds from the open doorways of other bars. I walked back to the hostel. I was lucky my assailants hadn't poked a finger at the bulges of my loose cotton t-shirt in the dim light of the strip club. Under the shirt, I was wearing my unusually small money belt like a long necklace. The flat cloth pouch on my chest held over two thousand baht and three credit cards.

6. TEMPLES AND DISH TOWELS

IN THAILAND, I was exposed to the human crush and diesel fumes of Asian buses, incessant girly-pop songs blaring from cheap radios, and inescapable noise from the two-stroke engines of *tuk-tuk* taxis and long-tail boats. I had learned to hold my breath and hurry past some noxious alleys in Bangkok. However, I discovered upon arrival that India, by comparison, was an all-out assault on the senses.

The southeastern city of Chennai, or Madras as it was known at the time, was congested with cars, trucks, three-wheeled taxis, motorcycles, bicycles, oxcarts, rickshaws, cows, and beggars. Many people walked the streets barefoot. Yet no matter how many vehicles and people filled the city road, there was always just barely enough room for the bus to squeeze through. I was battered on all sides by the sounds of honking horns, bicycle bells, touts calling "Hallo, hallo!" and beggars calling "Rupee, rupee!" When I asked my rickshaw driver why so many drivers kept honking their horns for no apparent reason, he cheerfully answered, "One must sound to alert others of your presence!"

Everywhere I looked I saw emaciated beggars in rags. The older ones sat wherever they were tolerated. They looked up mutely as you passed and raised a palm for donations. Or they would mime the motion of eating with one hand, while patting the empty belly with the other. The child beggars were bolder. These children would shamelessly approach and cling to your legs, reaching into your pockets while staring up at you with desperate eyes.

In the mornings, you would see men squatting on the railroad tracks, discretely spaced about ten feet apart in the multi-track railway yards. They were defecating in the open air. I don't know where the women did their business. Apparently, Tamil Nadu women complain that it takes up a good chunk of their time every day to look for an outdoor location with enough cover and privacy to relieve themselves.

The cow is a sacred animal in the Hindu religion. In this part of India, cows roamed the towns freely. You would find a few cows in every street, unconcerned by people or traffic, standing idly or munching stray tufts of vegetation. I could see no sign that anyone owned these cows, nor cared where they wandered. I never learned whether they had a home or a stall for the night. Veiled women in *saris* were collecting the cow dung from the roads. They formed it into burger-sized patties with their bare hands, and then stuck the patties up around the base of the trees lining the streets. Every tree trunk was decorated with a neat array of drying cow-turd patties. I guessed that the dried patties would be collected later for use as cooking fuel or fertilizer.

Young men walked the streets holding hands. It was a display of friendship rather than homosexuality. Personal space was non-existent. While I waited in a long snaking queue to buy a bus ticket, the young Indian fellow behind me casually draped his left arm over my left shoulder. As I glanced down at the intruding appendage on my left, the fellow then leaned his head forward over my right shoulder, his chest brushing up against my back. I'd reached the head of the line as the person before me stepped away. It was my turn in front of the glass booth. Bemused at first, I realized my new touchy-feely companion behind simply wanted to watch my transaction with the ticket seller.

I made my way south by bus through India's Tamil Nadu state, to visit the ancient temples along the coast of the Bay of Bengal. My first destination was a small town with the mellifluous name of Mahabalipuram.

A teenage tout met me at the Mahabalipuram bus station. As he approached, he said, "Hello, hello," as they all do, but in an unexpectedly mild and polite tone. He asked if I were looking for lodgings, and I nodded. He led me on a short walk to a small, free-standing cinder-block structure. The wooden door looked like it had been constructed from salvaged boards nailed together. Inside the single room was a thin cotton mattress on a concrete floor, illuminated by a bare incandescent light bulb dangling from the ceiling. There was one window with wooden shutters which could be secured from the inside. Except for the mattress, there was not another stick of furniture. There was a hose jutting out of the wall at eye level at the far corner, serving as a shower head. The concrete floor sloped down in that corner to a drain. There was neither a shower curtain nor wall tiles to demarcate a shower stall. Next to the shower, embedded in the cement floor, were the raised white ceramic foot supports and dark opening of a squat toilet.

Building a toilet is still a major cost today that most Tamil Nadu families cannot afford. Eight years after my visit, the government of India introduced a program providing subsidies for each household to construct a latrine. Government funding of this "Total Sanitation Campaign" was extended in 2004, with the goal of eliminating open-air defecation by 2019, the year of the one hundred and fiftieth birthday of Mahatma Gandhi. But by 2019, it looked like that goal was still a decade or more away. Cultural preferences, unreliable water supplies, and the tendency for the subsidies to be spent on other things have stymied the campaign.

I can't imagine living with the stress of needing to find an outdoor location to poop every single day. The cost of a night in that room in Mahabalipuram was five rupees, less than twenty cents Canadian. At least I wouldn't have to join the men squatting in the fields. I agreed to rent the room, paid my guide his commission, and settled in. There was only one faucet for the shower, but the water was pleasantly lukewarm in this season of thirty-five-degree heat. After showering, I set off to explore the town.

Mahabalipuram could very well be the stone-carving capital of the world. Each morning would start with a cacophony of crows, dogs, cows, and roosters greeting the daylight. Then the steady *clink clink* of metal tools chipping stone would begin. Stone chipping at over a dozen sheds about town did not stop until well into the night. Some of the shops had small hand-written signs in English, "Learn to carve stone in a few days," inviting tourists to take up the skill. Another traveler I met said a proper apprenticeship would actually take five years. That seemed likely, since the first thing you needed to learn was how to draw Hindu religious figures on the giant slabs of rock to guide the carving.

Stone carvers in Mahabalipuram, India.

At each covered workspace, grey granite blocks of various sizes stood in an adjoining yard, awaiting the chisel. The blocks came from quarries in Kanchipuram sixty-five kilometres inland to the west. The finished products would go to temples all over India or to museums worldwide. Other projects included commissioned sculpture enlargements from small originals sent by international artists. Needless to say, these skilled Indian workers were paid a distressingly low hourly wage. Despite flying stone chips and heavy rock workpieces, none of these craftsmen wore safety glasses while wielding hammer and chisel. Most were squatting or kneeling in bare feet, with their flip-flop footwear safely stowed in a corner. Obviously, part of the apprenticeship was learning how to hit the rock so that the stone chips fly away from your face, and not into your eyeballs.

At midday, I went looking for food. There was a pavilion serving as the local butcher shop in the market area. Very few of the windows in town had glass. They were instead fitted with wooden shutters. The butcher shop was no different. Hanging from the rafters and arranged on the counters were various lumps of black, glistening with the wings of crawling flies. I watched as a customer pointed to one of these lumps. The shopkeeper waved his hand to shoo away the flies. The meat passed the customer's inspection, and then there was a bit of haggling in what I assumed was the Tamil language.

After agreeing on a price, the butcher removed the carcass to slice off the requested portion, wrapped it up in waxed paper, and handed it to the customer for payment. The remaining chunk of meat was put back on display, and quickly disappeared under flies again.

I became an instant vegetarian for this portion of my trip.

I could not read Tamil, but it was easy to spot a restaurant. Men, single or in small groups, streamed into a line stretching down the block outside an open doorway to an eatery. For some reason, each man in the queue had what appeared to be a white-checkered dishtowel draped over one shoulder. I joined the line. Once I got inside the doorway, it looked like a North American charity soup kitchen. Staff was dispensing a ration of food to each customer from one of two big metal vats containing vegetable *biryani*. After getting a plate heaped high with white rice and veggies, the customer paid and sat down to eat at the cafeteria-style benches in the room.

When my turn came, I pointed to my choice and received rice, veggies, and a plastic cup full of water. I continued down the line to pay a few rupees. After I proceeded to find an unoccupied spot to eat, I realized I'd forgotten to pick up cutlery. That was when I registered that everyone in the room was eating with bare hands.

Have you ever tried eating sticky rice with your hands? With each handful, half would enter my mouth, and the other half would remain stuck on my fingers. In no time, my hand was encrusted in a glove of rice and diced vegetables. I repeatedly licked clean my fingers one by one, before trying to put another handful of biryani into my mouth. Stealing furtive glances at my Tamil neighbours, I saw that none of them seemed to have this problem. Everyone else in the place could skillfully roll up a ball of biryani on their fingertips and pop it into their mouths without a single grain of rice sticking to their skin. Maybe there was a spray-can of "non-stick" for hands somewhere in the restaurant?

After I emptied my bowl of biryani, my stomach was no longer grumbling but my hand was coated in rice residue and saliva. I had rice grunge under my fingernails. Now I saw that, as each man finished his meal, he lined up at a row of sink basins at the other side of the restaurant. There was no soap. Each guy would rinse his "food hand" under the tap, and then wipe dry with the dish towel draped over his shoulder.

I had arrived without a dish towel. At least they hadn't turned me away at the door.

The next morning, I took a taxi a short distance out of town to the ancient Hindu temple on the bay. The Shore Temple at

Mahabalipuram is five stories high and made of carved granite. Every day here began with a giant red sun rising out of the water in the east. The red light gives a warmth to the weathered granite temple. The elaborately carved stone structure was built around 700 CE by India's Pallava rulers, right on the beach, at a time when Mahabalipuram was a busy and flourishing port. Those days are long gone, but the temple is now a UNESCO World Heritage site. The Mahabalipuram temple is the only one remaining of the legendary or mythical "Seven Pagodas." Parts of the temple complex have been covered by the sea over the last 1,300 years.

Shore temple at Mahabalipuram, India,
viewed from the west with the beach and ocean behind.

Hinduism seemed to be more of a way of life than a religion. Hindu's believe in a continuous cycle of birth, life, death, and rebirth; enjoying pleasure from the senses, including food, sex, and music; social order and ethical behavior; and the goal of seeking wealth or prosperity. Unlike the one god of Jews, Christians, Muslims and Sikhs, there are thirty-three principal gods in Hinduism who sometimes interfere with the lives of human beings. Just for fun. Three of the most powerful Hindu deities are named Brahma, Vishnu, and Shiva, and they are responsible, respectively, for the creation, preservation, and destruction of the world. The god of destruction is not evil but rather the destroyer of evil. It is Shiva's job to destroy the world at the end of every age in preparation for world renewal. Shiva is also the god of dance.

While classical Greek temples are dedicated to a single god, one Hindu temple can contain shrines to several gods. The Mahabalipuram temple has two shrines dedicated to lords Shiva and Vishnu. I watched as dozens of tourists arrived to visit these shrines: Indian men in light button-front shirts and dark trousers; Indian women in brilliant vivid colorful saris; and busload after busload of Indian schoolchildren in uniform. They trooped through the temple's stone passageways, and then walked to the sand and waves of the adjacent beach. There were vendors at the beach selling shells, necklaces, wind chimes, sandals, flutes, postcards, slices of watermelon, and small stone carvings from Mahabalipuram town.

I purchased a cup of ice cream from a beach vendor. The vanilla ice cream was delicious, and I savored the cold treat while walking with the waves lapping over my bare toes in the summer sun. Every part of the sky was blue, as it had been since I'd landed in India. I had truly dodged the clouds by coming to this part of the world. After eating the ice cream, I looked around for a trash bin to dump the plastic-coated paper cup and plastic spoon. I walked along the beach, first in one direction and then another, towards objects that appeared to be garbage bins from a distance, but which turned out to be something else.

The man who had sold me the ice cream watched, amused, lounging in the partial shade of a large boulder. At length he approached. I realized this must be a common predicament for his customers on the beach. He was going to take the garbage from me to dispose of in town later. Gratefully, I handed him the used cup and spoon. He smiled at me. I saw that he wasn't missing any teeth, and they looked healthy. Then he turned and tossed the litter as far as he could out into the waves.

Over the next few days, I made my way further south through Puducherry to Chidambaram to visit the Great Temple of Nataraja, or Shiva as the Lord of Dance. Unlike the Mahabalipuram temple, which is more like a large stone sculpture, the Nataraja temple is a huge complex with many halls and interconnecting corridors. Large gateway towers, or *gopurhams*, provide entrances to the temple complex from the four cardinal directions. Each *gopurham* has seven tiers, reaches about 250 feet high, and is decorated with successive rows of carved statuettes from Hindu mythology.

Arriving at the entrance to the temple, I probably looked as lost as I felt. I was still wearing my backpack after the bus ride into town and then the rickshaw ride to the temple. The modern chain-link gates installed at the front entrance were now obviously closed. An Indian fellow trotted up and introduced himself as Panneer. He explained that the temple was closed for midday ceremonies until five p.m. Hindu rituals, services for worshippers, and the chanting of hymns, or *puja*, take place in a regular schedule throughout each day, led by Brahmin priests. When I informed Panneer that I could return at five o'clock, he said that westerners were not allowed in anyway.

Then, with a conspiratorial look, Panneer told me to take off my shoes and follow him in quickly. The gate was closed, but not locked. He held it open as I kicked off my sandals. We went in, closing the gate behind us. I moved with extra urgency now that my bare feet were burning on the stone courtyard slabs baking in the sun. I grew doubtful of the 'no westerners' rule when I was asked to leave my pack and shoes outside. Another Indian man was stationed there, obviously to watch over visitors' belongings. He was not at all surprised that I, a non-local, was going inside.

I followed Panneer as he ducked into the cool shadows of the ancient stone structure.

Once inside, Panneer became my tour guide. He proceeded to describe the history of the Nataraja Temple and some of the colorful pantheon of Hindu lore and religion. Panneer told me a story of how the oldest part of the Nataraja Temple was built by the first Chola emperor. That emperor was afflicted with leprosy, and he had travelled the land looking for a cure. He took a bath at a small pond in the forest with a shrine dedicated to Shiva. There, he encountered two mystical servants. The emperor recognized these servants as supernatural beings, because one had the body of a snake and the other had the feet of a tiger. When the emperor entered the water, he was cured of leprosy. Paneer's story was that this emperor built the first part of the Nataraja Temple at the site to demonstrate his gratitude to Shiva.

Panneer (foreground) inside the
Temple of Nataraja in Chidambaram, India.

Later, I learned that the exact origin of the Chidambaram temple seems, in fact, to have been forgotten. The temple already existed when it was used by Chola emperors in the second century CE. Indian scholars identified the emperor in Panneer's story as Emperor Simhavarman, who ruled much later during the fifth century CE. Simhavarman cured his leprosy by bathing in the Sivagangai tank. The tank was one of several stone pools or reservoirs already built on the Nataraja Temple grounds by the time Simhavarman arrived. In gratitude, Simhavarman made extensive repairs and renovations to the existing structures.

Panneer was probably recounting the legends of the temple as best as he could. I doubt very many of the tourists he shepherded through the site ever bothered to verify Panneer's version of the story, which was no less entertaining. Panneer knew that he would earn a tip as a temple tour guide as long as he entertained; historical accuracy was irrelevant.

With Panneer continuing as my guide, we proceeded through several connecting halls and corridors. Panneer offered to take a picture, using my camera, of me standing beside the Golden Pillar. This was an elaborately carved stone column in the temple that is coated with a layer of gold. The Golden Pillar was protected by a small metal cage on four sides up to eye level. When I asked why that specific column had been gilded, Panneer, sadly, had no explanation.

We moved on through more of the temple, passing walls and ceilings brightly painted with religious scenes or images of Hindu deities. We came to the second oldest part of the temple, the Nritta Sabha Hall. Panneer explained how this hall commemorated a dance contest between Shiva and a challenger, a lesser goddess known as Kaali. The stone stage in the hall was constructed to resemble a chariot, with a horse head protruding from the left side, and the top half of a wheel on the right. There are one hundred and eight carved figures on the stone columns around the room, which show Shiva in each of the one hundred and eight different dance positions, or *karanas*, of the Dance of Delight. Panneer enthusiastically described how the angry Shiva karana had his right leg and left arm up in the air, in contrast to the happy Shiva karana, where the left leg was raised, foot pointing to the right, and the arms are held out in front. Since Shiva's expression was identical on every column, it was not obvious to me how one position conveyed anger, while the other showed happiness. I guess that was because I am not a Hindu.

Shiva, of course, won the dance contest. Kaali was sent off to be the goddess of a minor temple on the outskirts of Chidambaram town.

The Nataraja Temple has been maintained and rebuilt over two thousand years through donations by various kings, rulers and wealthy individuals. Most recently, according to Panneer, the four *gopurhams* had each been repaired with donated money. He said that one gopurham was rebuilt from funds donated by Hawaiian tourists, one by Chidambaram University, one by a wealthy physician in Chennai, and the final tower by the Tamil Nadu government. *Technically*, I thought, *the last bit of funding was from local taxation rather than a donation.* I didn't say this to Panneer.

Occasionally I saw emaciated Brahmin priests, white-bearded Indian holy men dressed in plain white robes, wandering the corridors. One of these holy men approached me. He asked, in crisp perfect English, "Do you have a pen?"

Obliging, I reached into the pouch where I carried my camera and notebook. I retrieved a ballpoint pen and lent it to the priest. He held the writing instrument up to his eyes horizontally. With an end in each hand, he inspected the pen carefully with a slight smile. Then he said brightly, "Thank you!" He turned on his heel and walked away with my pen.

I think I just stood there with my mouth open in surprise. Panneer put a sympathetic hand on my shoulder, explaining, "It's just something the priests do."

After the tour of the Nataraja Temple, Panneer invited me back to his home for a late lunch. I accepted, retrieved my shoes and backpack, and walked with Panneer to his unassuming residence. We ate lunch outside, on stools and a small rough table set up in the paved backyard. I was served rice, tomatoes, and some unknown vegetable that looked like a cross between a cherry and a chili pepper, which tasted like squash. There was lemon curry soup. I made sure to eat everything with my right hand. The urban myth in Canada was that Indian people always reserved their left hands for wiping off after a bowel movement. I never asked anyone in India the pointed question of whether this was true.

The meal would have been quite enjoyable except that we were joined by Panneer's three very thin children and his very yellow wife. The causes of jaundice in adults include a blockage or tumor in the pancreas or bile ducts, and Hepatitis, which is an infectious disease. I had taken a Hepatitis B vaccine before commencing my travels, but I knew there were other forms of Hepatitis for which there was no vaccine back in 1991. I tried to not let my discomfiture show and ate the proffered food.

I made a small "donation" of fifty rupees to Paneer's family. The temple was not operated by the government but instead by three hundred Brahmin families, including Panneer's family. Brahmins are a Hindu caste, or social class, whose members traditionally become priests, scholars, and teachers. These Brahmin families are the beneficiaries of the centuries-old Chidambaram temple but they also have the burden of maintaining the stonework, vegetable-dye ceiling paintings, lighting, and plumbing, as well as feeding and clothing the Brahmin priests who lead the daily rituals. Apparently, I was the first western tourist in ten days and probably the last until the hot season was over. Panneer would not see any more donations for some time. It would be difficult for his family to get enough food until the tourists returned.

From Chidambaram, I continued to Tanjore, the ancient capital city of the Chola Empire (850-1270 CE). Then I went on to Madurai, where I enjoyed sugary tea on a rooftop with a Kashmiri salesman named Imtiaz. From Madurai, I boarded a train bound for Kolkata (formerly Calcutta) in the cooler north, over a thousand kilometres away.

The train ride to Kolkata provided ample time to ponder what would happen when I got back to Canada. Or would I be going back to Canada? I reread a letter from Mariana, which I had picked up from *Post Restante* in Bangkok. I thought seriously about a prolonged stay with her in Spain. Could I work in a Spanish shoe shop? I wrote a letter to mail back to Mariana at the first opportunity. In my letter, I tried hard to avoid being presumptuous.

By now, I had dismissed all notions of working as a diver. That had been one of the options I had entertained before leaving Canada. After seeing scuba-diving outfits in Fiji, Australia, and Thailand, I realized that dive masters were not exactly in high demand. More importantly, I realized that I would quickly grow tired of shepherding tourists on dive trips, and any resort in a tropical paradise would become a prison if I needed to stay there to earn a living. I couldn't see myself as an undersea welder, treasure hunter, or archeologist either.

I guess I'd really shot myself in the foot by quitting graduate school.

I remembered celebrating with friends in 1986, after we finished our undergraduate degrees at the University of Toronto. The music was loud, the girls were smokin' hot, and we were drunk and exorcising our exam demons on the dance floor. Errol was going to make a million bucks with his B.A. in Commerce, becoming CEO of a major Asian bank. Carson was going to see the world in style, flying business class with an international firm of chartered accountants. Marcus was going to discover the next subatomic particle at some physics institute in Germany. I was going to get a Ph.D., and then make my mark with a breakthrough in gene therapy at the biotech giant Genentech. I already knew I was going to break up with Amanda, my girlfriend at the time, and continue my path to graduate school in another city.

All my life I had been building towards that future. The plan was to first achieve academic success, then financial success, and finally career success. That's simply what every good son of hard-working Chinese immigrant parents did in Canada: get a university degree, become a respected bread-winner, and make a contribution to society. Who could have guessed that I, the introverted and academically successful science nerd, would find myself running away from basic life sciences research, after a few short years in the lab, because it was too socially isolating?

And just how was I going to make my mark now? What would be my goal, my motivation? Or at least get me out of bed in the mornings? Did I need to go back to square one and start a fresh undergraduate degree, far behind my peers? Was law school the answer? Maybe I should devote myself to saving the planet instead, and join some environmental non-government organization?

Three months into my round-the-world adventure and I was no further in deciding about my future.

7. SECOND-CLASS, THREE-TIER

ACCORDING TO THE traveler's grapevine, the way to go for backpacker train travel in India was "second-class, three-tier." Second class was cheaper than first-class air-conditioned compartments. "Three-tier" meant that each railcar had three levels of bunk beds, one above the other folding out from the train car wall. By all accounts, the money you would save by taking third class was not worth the discomfort of travel with no amenities in cattle-car conditions. I took second-class, three-tier on the train to Kolkata.

For forty-three hours, I was entertained watching family life on the train. Grandma was contentedly perched on the top berth, while Grandpa's skinny legs dangled from the middle berth. Mom and Dad played with Baby on the lowest berth, or rocked the baby in a make-shift hammock fashioned from sheets brought along for that purpose. This Indian family cautioned me to keep an eye on my belongings, because there were thieves on the train. In the evening, the young men in the railcar chatted and played cards, while the older passengers and women read magazines. At night, the temperatures cooled enough with the breeze blowing through the railcar to get a full night of sleep.

After every couple of hours, or when the train paused at a town, vendors walked down the aisles calling "Chai, chai, chai!" "Ka-fay, ka-fay, ka-fay!" "Ka-wality Ize Cream!" or "Om-led, egg! Om-LED!" These refreshments would be served on bio-degradable vessels. Beverages came in thin pottery cups, that looked like miniatures of the utilitarian orangey-brown ceramic pots used for gardening in Canada. Food came wrapped in a large green leaf, resembling a freshly cut tobacco leaf. No cutlery was used. When you were done eating or drinking, the pottery cups and leaves were simply tossed out the train windows, which were fitted with parallel horizontal steel bars instead of glass. The leaves decomposed, and the cups went back to dust on the train tracks. India was ahead of its time for sustainable food packaging.

The entire ride was uneventful, except when an Indian fellow discovered his wallet had been stolen. There were cries of consternation. Other passengers voiced outrage, but nothing was done, and the victim accepted his fate.

Indians are well-adapted to travel comfortably in "second-class, three-tier" mode. Over time, sweat and grime coated every passenger as warm air and dust blew in constantly through the windows. Each family in the railcar seemed to have an endless supply of tea towels to wipe off sweaty faces. Indian women wore saris or skirts, and Indian men wore *lungis*. A *lungi* or *sarong* is a traditional Indian garment for men that resembles a loose full-length skirt with a narrow elastic waist. Periodically, the male passengers would change out of sweaty, grimy pants and underwear beneath a lungi, which functioned as a portable privacy screen.

I was not Indian, and I was not so well-adapted. Slowly, inevitably, I became covered in rice and sauce splatter from inexpert eating with my fingers. I had no privacy lungi for changing, and my clothes turned black with air-borne dirt and stiff with dried sweat. It was unthinkable to change in the cramped and foul lavatory on the moving train. While hair on the Indian passengers looked the same before and after the journey, my hair looked and felt like someone had smeared tablespoons of grease into it. It was too hot to hide under my hat. By the end of nearly two days, I was the filthiest, smelliest, most disgusting person in that railcar.

The train finally came to a stop in Kolkata. I walked out uncomfortably with the weight of my backpack pressing a soiled sticky shirt to my skin. I located a hostel as quickly as possible, desperate for a shower and change of clothes. Oddly, once at the hostel, I discovered many of the other backpackers had arrived from similarly epic train journeys. Of my new acquaintances, one had travelled twenty-four hours from Varanasi, another had arrived after forty-eight hours from Chennai, and a third, Trevor, had come by train from Kanyakumari at the southernmost tip of India, enduring a whopping fifty-two hours!

Kolkata came with a new challenge: Water rationing was in effect. My laundry came back with a grey tinge on all my clothing, because the washerwomen didn't have enough fresh water for rinsing. Hotel showers were only available for half an hour sometime between five and six p.m. That meant everyone hung around the guesthouse beginning at five o'clock, testing the taps at the showers every ten minutes or so to see if any water flowed. There were two shower rooms per floor in the three-story building. If you were lucky enough to discover water pressure, you jumped in. There was only the honor system to ensure no one unfairly monopolized a shower before the flow of water ended for that day. Some backpackers proved to be not so honorable.

Trevor, however, was in the shower for less than ten minutes before he rapped on my door to let me know the shower was available. Trevor was a native of New Zealand. He had very pale skin, straight reddish hair, and stereotypical freckles. He favored loose cotton shorts, a t-shirt, and sandals. He looked like he should be on a sandy beach somewhere rather than wandering the grey concrete streets of Kolkata. He was a naturally quiet individual with a shy smile, but he was surprisingly confident. We swapped stories about the heat we had both endured in Tamil Nadu. Trevor never left the hostel without carrying at least a liter of water.

"At the Sun Temple at Konark, I ran out of water. I'll never let that happen again," he intoned solemnly, reliving unbearable hours of agony.

I explored the city with Trevor. We visited Kolkata's Eden Gardens, a public green space. Next, we enjoyed a few hours of air-conditioned comfort at the Birla Planetarium in the afternoon. Kolkata temperatures did not reach the mid-thirties of Tamil Nadu cities in the south, but Kolkata daytime heat still peaked at twenty-eight to twenty-nine degrees Celsius. In the cool darkness of the planetarium, the Indian operator of the telescope proudly rhymed off the names of about a thousand stars. After the planetarium, Trevor and I treated ourselves to dinner at the Fairlawn Hotel. The hotel still operated in the tradition of the British Raj. *Raj* means "rule" in Hindi. After the powerful British East India Company controlled the Indian subcontinent for a century, Britain took over and ruled for another ninety years. By the time the British left in 1947, formal English meal etiquette was firmly established. We were called to dinner by a server striking a gong. The costumed server in a fancy white turban attended our meal with bone china plates and fine silverware.

Server in the restaurant of the Fairlawn Hotel, Kolkata, India. A small dinner gong is suspended in a white frame behind the server's left arm.

The following afternoon, Trevor and I spent almost four hours at the sprawling Imperial Museum at Kolkata. Founded in 1814, it is the oldest and largest museum in India. The exhibition halls are filled with stone-temple fragments, Buddhist and Hindu statuettes, page-sized contemporary Indian paintings, reams of musty woven fabrics, colossal animal skeletons, furry animal displays from the "shoot and stuff" epoch, shelves crammed with rock samples, and panels of pinned insects. The museum boasts a fabulous Egyptian room, and—most intriguing—a great hall devoted to lifestyles of the dozens of modern-day Indian tribes.

I was surprised to learn in the museum's Cultural Anthropology Gallery that, just like the United States of America and the United States of Mexico, India is also a country consisting of united states. The states of India include Tamil Nadu, West Bengal, Rajasthan, Punjab, and so forth. In all, there are twenty-nine states and seven territories in India, governed by a parliamentary system. Each Indian state has a capital, such as the mega-cities of Delhi, Kolkata, and Mumbai, and a thousand under-developed thatch-hut villages linked by bus routes. The villages are home to indigenous Indian tribes with populations of 150 souls to over 200,000 people.

One of the displays in the anthropology gallery explained how, on an Indian island in the Andaman Sea, inhabitants used coconut shells for cups, and relied on finding shards of glass that wash up on the beach to fashion cutting tools. At first, I thought this was an archaeological exhibit. Then I realized it was describing an Indian society of the 1990s on one of the country's remote islands.

To this day, the tribe on India's North Sentinel Island has remained hostile to the modern world. The tribe has lived on the island for an estimated 60,000 years, and its people throw spears at outsiders who try to make contact. The islanders have killed foreign fishermen who ventured too close. In 2004, a tsunami hit the island. After the devastation, the Government of India sent a helicopter with food and supplies to help. The helicopter was greeted with a shower of rocks and arrows from the first islanders who spotted it. In 2018, a young American man paid for fishermen to smuggle himself to the island. He wanted to show the islanders the way to Jesus. Once on the island, armed tribesmen with yellow paste smeared on their faces killed the missionary and buried him on the beach. The North Sentinelese may be the last "untouched" indigenous people on the planet.

8. THE LITTLE ENGINE THAT COULD

THE LITTLE TRAIN to Darjeeling went up and up into the clouds. Unfortunately, those clouds and fog obscured any view of the surrounding mountains. I never did catch a glimpse of Kanchenjunga, the third highest mountain in the world, but the cooler temperatures were a refreshing change from the sweltering plains below. Houses in the towns we passed appeared progressively better kept with increasing elevation. In contrast to the tired utilitarian houses in Siliguri, where the train had started, more and more of the private homes as we climbed featured tidy drapes, potted plants, and even welcome mats in some of the doorways.

Before boarding the train to Darjeeling, I had first taken a bus with Trevor from Kolkata to Siliguri. I was crammed in the middle of the bus bench seat, with Trevor on my right and a young Indian man on my left. All men are not created equal. My right arm was drenched by Trevor's sweat. Although he carried a New Zealand passport, Trevor obviously had United Kingdom sweat glands, probably from Irish ancestors. On the bus, Trevor was rehydrating continuously from two water bottles, but it was like pouring water into a burlap sack. I kept leaning away from him. My own skin was glistening with perspiration but producing nowhere near the gushing waterfall of Trevor. On my left, however, the Indian guy was talcum powder dry. I could see the toned brown, moisture-free skin on his arm as *he* kept pulling away from *me*.

The temperature did not cool significantly even when we arrived in Siliguri. From here, Trevor and I parted. Trevor opted to stay a few days in Siliguri town, while I chose to enter the clouds on the toy train up to Darjeeling.

The locomotive on the Darjeeling Himalayan Railway (DHR) is literally a toy train. The miniature train travels on a two-foot narrow-gauge railway and uses "zigzag and loop line" technology invented in the 1800s. The track turns around in loops, and zigzags where the direction of the train reverses, in order to climb the steepest sections of the route. From New Jalpaiguri Station at Siliguri, the train takes seven and a half hours and makes twelve stops before reaching Darjeeling at the top. The elevation gain is more than two kilometers, from 100 meters above sea level to about 2,200 meters.

The DHR train has been running since 1881. It was built by the Eastern Bengal Railway Company during the British Raj, largely to transport tea and wealthy British vacationers. The DHR is now operated by Indian Railways (a government agency). The original steam engines have been replaced by modern diesel engines. The DHR was declared a UNESCO World Heritage feature in 1999, eight years after I rode the railway up into the mountains.

As the engine strained up the grade, in my head I heard, *I think I can, I think I can, I think I can*, from the children's story *The Little Engine That Could*. The DHR toy train was even painted light blue, just as on the illustrated hard cover of the storybook I remembered as a child.

Although Darjeeling is still in India, the local faces we saw from the train were clearly more Tibetan or Chinese than Indian. As the train slowed through each town, school children in uniform ran and leapt onto the railcars. They found footholds on the lower exterior and thrust their elbows through the bars on the windows to steady themselves. You could hear how this burden further strained the tiny engine. Each group of children would cling to the outside of the train for a few minutes before hopping off as they neared their family homes, stealing a ride for part of the distance coming back from school.

Eventually, the train pulled itself into Darjeeling Station, and I hoisted my pack in cool air to find the next guesthouse. Everywhere in the city, I saw reminders of China's occupation of Tibet. Since China invaded in 1950, unhappy Tibetans have fled south across Tibet's border with Nepal, Bhutan, or India. Many of those who crossed into India's Sikkim State continued south to find work in Darjeeling. These Tibetan refugees are treated as stateless persons. Most do not have Indian passports, not even Tibetan children born in India. It also seems that the vast majority of Tibetan refugees have no desire to integrate with Indian society.

I stopped in a Tibetan coffee shop in Darjeeling. Inside was a framed wall-hanging that read, "Tears are the hydraulic force by which masculine will power is defeated." Right next to that framed statement were posters of Conan the Barbarian (Arnold Schwarzenegger) and Rambo (Sylvester Stallone), two hyper-male characters from Hollywood action movies. I didn't know if putting that phrase next to those posters was intended to convey a message of some kind.

I went on a tour of the Tibetan Refugee Self-Help Centre in Darjeeling. The centre focused on training new Tibetan arrivals to make and sell Tibetan handicrafts, and hence the building is named to emphasize self-help. For a Tibetan refugee in India, the general alternative to working as an artisan is to scrape by as an unskilled laborer. My father taught me the old Chinese saying, "*Mo chen; Mo mieng,*" which translates to "No money; no life."

At the entrance to the Self-Help Centre, a Tibetan woman greeted me with a friendly smile. She said, "*Konichi-wa?*" meaning hello in Japanese. I knew she meant well and returned her smile.

Only women were present in the centre, and all of them wore the traditional Tibetan multicoloured aprons made of connected small striped squares. Apparently, the apron pattern indicates whether the wearer was married, and what village she came from. I saw several women working wooden looms, producing Tibetan-style fabric.

Woman weaving traditional Tibetan cloth in Darjeeling, India.

The Self-Help Centre in Darjeeling still operates today, thirty years after my visit. The centre's handicrafts are sold worldwide now through the internet. Products include carpets, carved wooden items, clothing, and woolen hats, mitts, and scarves. Success has meant demand outstrips supply for the centre's high-quality Tibetan carpets that emphasize intricate traditional patterns. The standard waiting period for a carpet order is one year.

Most North Americans, however, would not associate Darjeeling with Tibetans, but with tea. Along with Earl Grey and English Breakfast, Darjeeling tea was a staple for me growing up in Toronto, Canada. When the British first arrived in Darjeeling, there were only about a hundred indigenous inhabitants on the mountainside. But then, in the 1840s, the British brought tea seeds from China, discovered that the hills around Darjeeling were perfect for growing tea bushes, and the rest is history. No visit to Darjeeling is complete without touring a tea farm.

I joined a group of backpackers for a guided tour of the Happy Valley Tea Plantation, Darjeeling's second oldest tea estate established in 1854. The 440-acre plantation consisted of rolling hillsides covered by the tea bush *Camellia sinensis*. All tea comes from the same plant, but like wine grapes, there are different "varietals" of the tea bush. Most of the characteristics that distinguish one tea from another result from the unique soil and climate where the plant is grown, and from the way the leaves are picked and processed. On the tour, we saw the Happy Valley process for the plucked tea leaves and buds to be withered, rolled, and sorted. Tea-bush production declines with the age of the plant. The tour guide said that the plantation owners were concerned that most of bushes at Happy Valley were by then already half a century old, with some plants over a hundred years old.

Towards the end of the tour, we were shown the tea-leaf sorting room. A thick canvas sheet covered almost the entire concrete floor in the dimly lit room. A large pile of dried tea leaves was in the middle of the canvas. Four Indian women dressed in *saris* of drab grey or black sat cross-legged on the floor around the pile. Each woman had a wide, shallow wicker basket with a flat lid that also functioned as a tray. On these trays, these women were picking individual tea leaves or broken leaves out of the pile, sorting them into first grade (whole end bud), second grade (whole new leaf), third grade (whole larger leaves) and fourth grade (broken leaves). The powdered tea left over is not exported but used for local consumption. I can never drink tea anymore without picturing these four women.

Women sorting tea leaves in Darjeeling, India.

Later that day, the small group of travelers I had joined went up the road to the Darjeeling Planters' Club. It was started in the 1860s as a "black-tie club" for plantation owners and their wives. At the time of my visit, backpackers could buy inexpensive temporary memberships, and we didn't need to wear tuxedos or ties to enjoy the club perks.

After a dinner with brandy, we backpackers adjourned to a private room in the club and performed that age-old traveler's ritual: passing the joint. The room was falling apart, with cracks showing in some places on the plaster walls, but the old Victorian-style chairs were holding up well. We were a group of eight, including Brits, Aussies, Americans, one Scandinavian, and one Canadian (respectively, Cheryl and Collin, Kate and Nick, Cindy and Bruce, Anneliese and myself).

The 'joint' was the international currency of friendship: a hand-rolled cigarette paper filled with marijuana, *Cannabis sativa*, "Mary Jane," "weed," or "pot." This was in the days before the marijuana plant had been genetically manipulated to increase the content of its intoxicating ingredient, THC (tetrahydrocannibol). It was also long before Canadian politicians agreed to legalize recreational marijuana use nationally, and before several individual American states were also legalizing it, flouting American federal law. We sat in a circle and slowly, methodically, passed the smoldering joint, inhaling social tokes of the smoke. Many people smoke weed for social bonding and generating empathy within a group, rather than just to get high. The effects of smoking weed? Time seems to slow down. Worries fade away, and you feel like you can leave your own body and observe yourself. You start to believe you are announcing incredibly insightful revelations about yourself and the persons around you.

And then we had another joint. It was a pleasurable way to pass the time and trade backpacker stories.

9. THE ROOF OF THE WORLD

IT WAS DAY TWO of my trek to Sagarmatha National Park in Nepal, and I was sick and tired. Two days earlier, I had unfortunately eaten tainted food in Kathmandu. All throughout India for weeks before, I had fastidiously, unfailingly disinfected my drinking water with iodine pills. I had avoided meat at most Indian eateries. Then, the minute I'd left India, at the first restaurant in Nepal with a European appearance, I made the typical tourist mistake of eating a delicious Wiener schnitzel. Wise travelers know that the kitchens on Freak Street in Kathmandu are still operated with Nepalese standards of hygiene. I was not wise.

In addition to the food poisoning, there was no doubt that I was suffering the consequences of my own stupidity: I began this mountain trekking after weeks of inactivity. I had just spent countless hours sitting on Indian buses and trains and wandering at a snail's pace through Hindu temples and historic ruins. That was not the recommended training for the grueling physical challenge of Nepal.

In contrast to forced confinement on a train or a bus, trying to move as little as possible in the heat of India, trekking in Nepal is the act of walking. More precisely, it is walking an endless natural winding stairway formed by dirt, tree roots, and boulders, continuously uphill or downhill for hours at a time. While carrying a backpack containing all your worldly possessions. The rocks and stepping stones appeared to be both naturally occurring and placed by humans to afford a rough step-by-step ascent. You simply shoulder your backpack and go up, up, up, or down, down, down, through forests of blue pine trees and giant rhododendron bushes. For hours. The elevation gain, or loss, is usually up to 1,000 meters (3,280 feet) per day. There is shockingly little flat land in the Himalayan foothills.

I was trekking with two Americans, Jonathan and Kevin, and an Israeli fellow, Doron. My three travelling companions were in peak physical condition. All three of them had exercised and trained diligently in their home countries before flying to Nepal for this expedition. Ugh. I gritted my teeth and did most of the listening during the conversation on the trail.

We took breaks and meals at teahouses strategically spaced along the route. A teahouse is a traditional wooden Nepali family home, with an area to serve food for sale, and a large room containing rough beds or sleeping mats for overnight patrons. Usually available were tea, soft drinks (Coca-Cola, Fanta, and Sprite had cornered the market), *dhal bhaat* (lentil porridge), *chapattis* (a flatbread), and sometimes boiled eggs. These inexpensive teahouses dotted all the popular trekking routes in Nepal, and the teahouse staff spoke enough English to serve their tourist clientele. Trekking was popular with shoe-string-budget travelers, because unless you opted to hire a guide or a porter to carry your pack, there was nothing to spend money on except at these inexpensive teahouses. It was considered impossible to get lost on the well-marked trails. Few backpackers elected to hire guides for the main routes in Sagarmatha (Everest) park in the east, or for the Annapurna Circuit in the west. In fact, by 1991, the route around the Annapurna peaks was already widely derided as the "Coca-Cola Circuit" because so many guesthouses and cafes had sprung up to serve that popular, scenic, and less arduous trekking area.

The Nepali government required tourists to purchase trekking permits, limiting visits in the designated areas to thirty days. In practice, this time limit was rarely inconvenient and probably never enforced. I think the permits were just a government cash grab. Although I can't be certain that there were no public services in the trekking parks funded by these permits, we never saw a single Nepali official who could have been a park ranger or trail-maintenance staff.

Despite the thirty-day limit, most visitors were lucky to complete even one of the main routes anyway. This was because of three trek-terminating afflictions: food poisoning, knee problems, and altitude sickness.

Every traveler reads about altitude sickness before visiting Nepal. The sickness is caused by the decreased atmospheric pressure at high elevation. Even though the composition of air remains about 21 percent oxygen from sea level to a hundred kilometres up, decreased air pressure at higher altitude reduces the body's ability to absorb that oxygen through lung tissue into blood. This causes all sorts of unpleasantness like nausea, coughing, vomiting, brain swelling, and ultimately death. There is no way to predict when altitude sickness will affect a particular person, and it doesn't matter whether you are physically fit or have previously visited high altitudes without getting the sickness. There is no reliable way to avoid it, and no remedy except to descend immediately. Very often, physically fit trekkers arrive in Nepal, grow impatient and start trekking without first taking the time to acclimatize to the elevation, and then find their adventure ended prematurely by altitude sickness.

From Kathmandu, I decided to take the bus east to Jiri at the end of the road, literally, and proceed on foot. This would maximize time to acclimatize to the elevation gain, reducing the likelihood of altitude sickness. I became fast friends with one of my trekking companions, Jonathan, on that bus from Kathmandu. We both decided to head towards a lookout point on the peak of

Gokyo Ri, rather than follow the majority of trekkers who aimed for Everest Base Camp.

Both Jonathan and I had arrived for the posted four a.m. departure time at the Ratna Bus Park in Kathmandu. Nepali buses are designed for Lilliputians. My 5'8" frame barely squeezed into a seat. My hip was jammed against Jonathan on my right and the bus window on my left. Jonathan was about the same height and build as me. We two sat crammed together in the pre-dawn darkness for perhaps twenty minutes before realizing the bus was not about to leave anytime soon.

Outside in the growing light, cargo was being hoisted up onto a metal cage installed around the roof of the bus. Up went sacks of potatoes, coils of rope, copper pipe and wires, wooden crates, cardboard cartons of canned food, crates of bottled soft drinks, and bales of unknown commodities. After the roof was stacked high with goods, we watched as local Nepali men climbed up the ladder at the back of the bus, staking out seats on top of the jumbled cargo.

I exchanged a look with Jonathan. "What do you think?" I asked.

"Can't be worse than being inside with the chickens for four hours," Jonathan replied, grinning.

The two of us retrieved our packs and climbed up the back outside the bus. I promptly found a perch on top of a sack of potatoes, camera in hand. We would enjoy stunning views from up there. It would also be easier to keep an eye on our backpacks by having them next to us on the roof.

It was one of the most spectacular rides in my life. The bus wended to Jiri around spaghetti-noodle roads and hairpin turns up the mountains, ever higher towards the "Roof of the World." We progressed from steamy terraced rice fields and stands of bamboo to cool but humid tea plantations, and finally up into dry alpine forests. Frequently the edge of the road was less than a foot away from the outer tires. There were no guardrails at the crumbling lips of those sheer drops. It seemed against the laws of nature to have so many near-vertical mountainsides defying the forces of erosion.

Looking down over the precipices, our vertigo increased with the sway of the bus made top-heavy by the combined mass of humans and merchandise on the roof. Twice, we spotted bus carcasses rusting and abandoned far below the cliffs down which they had tumbled.

Jonathan and I speculated on what we would discover on the trails. We took inventory of the equipment we each had brought. I lamented my ridiculously heavy pack but was thankful for my boots. Jonathan had arrived with virtually no excess equipment, as he had flown to Nepal directly from his home in Boston and would be going home immediately after the trek. He had purchased a pair of fluffy red, down-filled mittens in Kathmandu. I had bought a blue light-weight down jacket that I hoped would be enough to keep me warm. I also confessed that I was carrying from Canada a portable propane stove, a small tent, and binoculars.

The air on the road to Jiri was fresh and the scenery glorious. We passed weird, stark trees dotting the hillsides, looking similar to the Joshua trees of the California desert. At various points along the highway, the bare rock faces of the fold mountains were exposed, revealing sedimentary rock layers that had actually *curled* from slow and massive tectonic forces working over geological time. The visual evidence of such unimaginable pressure over an unimaginable span of time made me feel very insignificant.

At each town that we passed, we saw home-made poster-board signs and suspended mobiles resembling paper lanterns that advertised political parties. Nepal was about to have its first-ever democratic elections. Most of the Nepali population was illiterate. For that historic first vote of 1991, the vying parties had each adopted a distinct hand-drawn symbol for political campaigning. Rather than proclaiming the virtues of the National Democratic, Nepali Congress, or Communist Party, the signs exhorted the masses to vote for the "tree," "cow," or "sun" party.

I read English-language newspapers with interviews of the political candidates. This was when I realized that Canadians enjoy a luxury that I think most are not even aware of. In the interviews, the Nepali political contenders said they would respect the democratic results and accept the governing decisions of the election winners. Unless those decisions were wrong; in which case the opposition vowed to fight the elected government in the streets. In Canada, we take for granted that the election losers will only fight the election winners verbally in Parliament. And we also assume the election winners will simply give up power when it is time for the next election. By 2019, the political leaders of China, Venezuela, and Egypt had all decided it was best for them to extend their own time in power.

When the bus stopped for rest breaks, Jonathan and I were surprised that other fellow trekkers steadfastly chose to stay inside, crammed into their seats. Better to die taking a chance and jumping off the top of the bus, we thought, than to be trapped inside going over the edge. However, after travelling almost 200 kilometres, the bus managed to reach Jiri without mishap.

From Jiri, Jonathan and I went to get lunch at a café. Inside, we sat down at a table where Doron and Kevin were already eating and became acquaintances. We started out as a party of four that same afternoon, heading towards Namche Bazaar in the east. The major rivers between Jiri and Namche run north-south, separated by high ridges. As a result, the trail going from west to east is basically a series of steep climbs and drops. By the end of day one we had walked to the village of Sangbadanda. By day two, Jonathan and I were lagging, while Doron and Kevin seemed unstoppable. Jonathan experienced worsening nausea, stomach cramps, and diarrhea, while my legs felt more and more like lead, and I had my own stomach troubles. At a midday rest break, we decided to hire porters at least until stopping for the second night.

DANCE WITH THE CLOUDS

Being a porter is the employment of last resort for a Nepali national. You were a porter if you couldn't find work as a farmhand, teahouse staff, or trekking guide. Boys as young as ten could be seen practicing and strengthening neck muscles by carrying boulders. Each boy leans forward and walks with a flat slab of rock tethered onto his back with a "tumpline", a cloth strap wrapping under the cargo behind and looping up in front around the forehead. Adult porters, all male, transported goods throughout the trekking trails using tumplines to carry loads of up to 150 pounds, sometimes with only flip-flops on their feet. The price of a bottle of Coca-Cola rises proportionately with elevation gain, because a porter was paid to carry that bottle up to the teahouse, and another porter would be paid to carry the empty bottle back down.

Hiring a porter was easy. Porters congregated at the same teahouses as trekkers, either resting *en route* with existing burdens, or waiting for casual employment by passing tourists. We were able to hire a group of four porters headed in our direction of travel, towards the village of Bhandar. These porters were eager to take on our baggage, even though they already had dauntingly large loads. We watched in amazement as each of these Nepali men expertly threw our packs up on top of their existing burdens, securing them with additional straps they magically produced from their pockets.

Without my backpack, I was able to keep up with Doron and Kevin. Barely. Jonathan also struggled, looking pale. The doubly-burdened porters had no trouble walking ahead, pausing occasionally for us to catch up. Conversation along the trail covered every topic imaginable. One of the pleasures of international travel is to learn about weird and unlikely things that are commonplace for someone living in another country. We talked about fruit. I mentioned that I had tried an unusual fruit called a prickly pear I discovered in the Kathmandu markets. Doron informed me the prickly pear was a common and popular fruit in Israel. He said that it was fitting, because the fruit resembled a hand grenade. Nearly all of Israel's eighteen to twenty-two-year-olds, both men and women, fulfill compulsory military service to protect the country from Arab threats.

Late in the afternoon, we parted ways with the porters. They were taking a path branching off to Bhandar while we continued towards Deurali. With payment and thanks, I also liberated myself from the weight of several large chocolate bars I had been carrying as emergency food. The candy bars were obviously redundant with so many teahouses along the route. I handed out the four large bars to the porters. Grateful, each porter wolfed down his chocolate on the spot in seconds. Then, smiling, they dropped the torn paper and foil wrappers to the ground, and promptly disappeared down the fork in the trail.

Our group of four trekkers continued walking through rhododendron forest as the sun dipped towards the horizon. We passed the occasional herd of yaks, rushing streams, and well-worn bridges. Up, up, up, or down, down, down. After about two hours, we heard the sound of running feet coming up from behind us.

One of the porters we had hired earlier approached, breathless and smiling. Without a word, he handed Doron an un-opened plastic bottle of drinking water. Apparently, the porters had entered Bhandar village and discovered Doron's water mistakenly still tucked within their other cargo. This Nepali porter had just travelled over two hours to overtake us and return that bottle. We were both impressed and disturbed by these actions. It was an impressive display of honesty, and disturbing that a seventy-five-cent bottle of water was valuable enough to the porter that he made such an effort to return it.

Eventually we arrived at the village of Deurali to spend the night. However, on the morning of day three, I was about to announce to my friends that my legs had given out. My pride was saved by Jonathan, who had become so ill with fever that it was clear he needed to recover in bed. While Doron and Kevin were impatient and elected to continue trekking without us, I stayed behind with Jonathan, silently thankful for at least one more day to get my legs into shape.

After seeing off Doron and Kevin that morning, I hung around the teahouse with the children of the owners. The boy, Radu, was about five, and his younger sister, Shu-Sheila, about three. I affectionately nicknamed them "Radical Dude" and "Sushi-La." I taught them the high-five, hand-slapping routine: Give me five (slap), up high (slap), down low (snatch away hand), too slow. I was working with them on their English ABCs and numbers when a couple of local Nepali men entered the teahouse. We exchanged the usual greeting, *Namaste,* and one of the pair, who spoke English well, struck up a conversation.

Radu (left) and Shu-sheila (right) with their family in Deurali, Nepal.

He was named Kalya, and he generally found employment as a trekking guide. No doubt he was able to access that higher paying job through his superior English language skills. After some chit chat, I learned that today was the Nepali New Year's Day, *Nawa Barsha*. Nepal celebrates the new year in April, based on the ancient *Bikram Sambat* calendar of Hinduism. Kalya invited me to join a local celebration lunch.

Leaving Jonathan asleep in bed at the teahouse, I was soon with a small group of Nepali villagers walking for an hour up to a grassy helipad, the nearest almost-flat clearing available for a picnic. Despite their easy-going interactions with international trekkers, Nepali society was tightly constrained by taboos between men and women. All the local men were dressed in western trousers, shirts, and jackets. A couple of the men sported sunglasses. The local women in our party, by contrast, were all wearing traditional garb with their patchwork woven aprons. Not only were public displays of affection between men and women taboo, it was unacceptable for an unmarried couple to be seen in public without a chaperone. Headed towards the picnic site, the men walked in a group, followed by a space and then the women in a separate group. At the clearing, someone brought out a battery-powered tinny-sounding radio. The women prepared the food for serving while the men lazed about, no doubt discussing important matters and making serious decisions.

Then the dancing began. First the men danced together, alternately waving their hands in the air and swaying and pirouetting, then holding hands and linking arms, moving slowly in a circle. I was asked to join the circle and demonstrate western dance. Let me just say that it is difficult to perform typical North American nightclub-style dance moves to the rhythm of Nepali New Year's music. Then someone put on a cassette tape of 1970s disco music. Again, my western dancing demo was an epic fail.

Celebrating Nawa Barsha in Nepal.
The author is in the centre of the dancing circle.

After the women's group had danced, we all sat in a large circle on the grass for the meal. I was served *chhang*, a white, low-alcohol beer with a sour smell made by fermenting rice. We enjoyed fresh yak's milk cheese, rice curry with dried grains, plain *chapattis*, and chicken broth soup.

My hosts peppered me with questions about how I earned a living in Canada. It was difficult to describe, because the Nepalis were not familiar with the concept of graduate school, where you were a student but funded through a university scholarship or a government grant. I settled for explaining that I was like a junior teacher, deriving a small salary through teaching-assistant duties.

More problematic was explaining the mystery of international currency exchange rates. You could work in Canada and earn two hundred Canadian dollars a day. In a typical Canadian city in 1991, that would be enough to pay the daily cost of food, clothing, rent, heating, electricity, public transportation, insurance, and entertainment. Yet, at thirty Nepali rupees to the Canadian dollar, that was equivalent to 6,000 rupees, a hefty sum that was far more than most Nepalis could earn in a month. To earn so much money, my hosts reasoned that Canadians must be superhuman, able to work a hundred times harder than a Nepali person in a single day. Canadians, they figured, probably never took time off to sleep, working 24/7 to accumulate so much wealth.

By the morning of day four, Jonathan's fever had broken, and he had recovered enough to continue east from Deurali. To our grateful beaming hostess, I gifted my camp stove, kerosene supply, and several packages of instant noodles, further lightening my load. I took a deep breath, hoisted my pack, and set off again with Jonathan.

We worried constantly about altitude sickness. I developed a mild but persistent cough. Our knees were also beginning to suffer pain and soreness. My right patella clicked each time I straightened my leg on a big uphill step. We crossed the bridge at the Likhu Khola River (1,543 meters) and walked up over 1,000 meters to the village of Sete (2,575 m). After a long day, we arrived not completely healthy but doggedly determined.

On day five, we continued from Sete up almost another 1,000 meters to complete the longest climb of the route so far, reaching Lamjura La pass (3,530 meters). At the pass, we experienced the peculiar sensation of not getting enough oxygen, despite sucking back deep breaths and walking slowly. The sunny weather held as we kept trekking through forests of fir, oak, pine, and massive rhododendron bushes. The area was home to monkeys, martens, and the small Himalayan musk deer, but we did not see any of these timid animals.

Jonathan and I had wide-ranging conversations, typical of solo backpackers becoming chance travel mates. We talked about religion. Jonathan summed it up: "Religion. It's highly personal."

I was reading the Bible at the time. I had just finished the four accounts of the Gospel. There was always a Bible in hotel rooms where I had stayed over the years in Canada, but this was the first time I was putting in the effort to read the book from cover to cover. Jonathan was a devout Christian, and his knowledge of Biblical passages was impressive. As an atheist, I had nothing but skeptical, albeit good-natured, questions for Jonathan.

"The King James version of the Bible," I stated, "is a version of the same stories that were first written down from the distant past. Why has nothing been added to the Bible in over two thousand years?"

"Simple," Jonathan replied. "Because it's complete. There's nothing more to be said."

Over the following days, the weather continued to be fantastic, with no rain and clear blue skies. Temperatures held steady in the low twenties Celsius. Hearty meals at teahouses included instant noodle soup, fried potatoes, rice with green onions, Sherpa stew, chapattis, cinnamon buns, and hot lemon drinks. The tea houses dotting the trekking route were welcome sights. My nights, however, were interrupted by abdominal pain. As a precaution, I swallowed some of the antibiotic pills I had brought in my emergency kit.

After leaving Junbesi, we caught our first glimpses of Mount Everest. Pausing near the village of Nunthala, we saw the highest mountain in the world rising up behind a range of closer peaks. Grey clouds were clinging to the eastern edge of Everest in what I imagined to be a super cold wind.

We continued trekking through rockslides with tricky footing, pine forests filled with the sounds of birds, apparently wild horses, and yet more stands of giant rhododendrons. This late into the dry season, there were no blooms in the rhododendron forest. We came to a great cleft rock with the thundering Dudh Khosi River a thousand feet below. We crossed by means of a long suspension bridge over the spectacular drop-off. We walked on through Moshe, a beautiful pastoral village filled with Buddhist stupas and cairn-like houses. After moving steadily east from Jiri, our route now turned due north following the 90 degree curve of the Dudh Khosi River. We would be following this same river valley all the way to our end point at Gokyo Ri. Marching through temperate forest past Lukla, we arrived at the village of Ghat (2,545 m) to spend the night.

On day eight, we set out from Ghat and at last entered the boundaries of Sagarmatha National Park at Jorsale. From here, we would continue north through blue pine forest to Namche Bazaar. Namche is the commercial centre for intrepid souls attempting the climb up Everest. Namche began as a trading post, where salt from Tibet was exchanged for grain from the south. Namche was full of shops run by Sherpas, an ethnic group that had migrated from Tibet into the Himalayas of Nepal in the 1400s. In 1991, only the towns of Namche and Lukla had electricity in this trekking region. Jonathan and I encouraged each other uphill with talk of Namche's bars, restaurants, and hotels with hot showers.

After an hour-and-a-half ascent which felt far longer, Namche finally came into view: an improbable town with hotels and museums tucked into a canyon at the top of a mountain. The skies became overcast in the late afternoon. As we entered the outskirts of town, we saw, incredibly, that quite a few tents had been set up by other trekkers. I could not fathom why any international tourist would sleep in a tent here, with such inexpensive guesthouse beds available. If you could afford to fly to this country, you could afford a few Nepali rupees for a hotel room. Jonathan and I chose a modest two-story guesthouse in town and treated ourselves to the luxury of hot baths. They were our first baths since leaving Kathmandu.

After getting ourselves clean and into fresh clothes, we left the hotel in the early evening to explore. In Namche, life was surreal with the contrast between local Nepalis walking around in flip-flops and sneakers full of holes, and the shops selling ultra high-tech, high-end climbing gear. You could buy all sorts of quality gear abandoned by wealthy international mountain climbers who didn't want to pack it for their homeward journey. We found a number of bakery cafes with chocolate cake on the menu, but we were unable to find aspirin for sale anywhere. In the streets, we encountered wandering yaks. That night, we had yak steaks for dinner, and I wondered if my dinner had once been a local resident.

It was highly advised for trekkers to stay an extra day in Namche Bazaar to acclimatize and reduce the chances of getting altitude sickness. My nagging cough had not gone away, and I was certain it was caused by the altitude. I mentally crossed my fingers and hoped my symptoms would not get worse. Fortunately, there was plenty to do in Namche to keep my mind off my symptoms. I went to visit the Everest Hotel, the highest hotel in the world; Sagarmatha National Park Visitor Centre, with displays on how Sir Edmond Hillary and his trusty Sherpa, Tenzing Norgay, were the first to reach the top of Mount Everest in 1953; and the Sherpa Cultural Museum, where I learned all about the Sherpa tradition of having serial wives.

One afternoon, Jonathan and I found ourselves again sucking as much air as possible into our lungs, straining to extract the oxygen. We were on a path returning from the Sherpa Cultural Museum, which was located on a ridge east of the town. A Tibetan woman had just appeared on the road behind us, driving a laden yak in front of her. We made each other a bet that we could maintain a walking pace to stay ahead of this woman. Despite valiant efforts, with Jonathan and I urging each other to walk faster, the Tibetan woman gradually, inexorably caught up. We could see no evidence that she was in a hurry, either. As she and her yak passed us, we collapsed to the ground in uncontrollable laughter, which made it even more difficult in our struggle to breathe.

On a disturbing note, when Jonathan and I arrived back in town from the museum, we discovered our one-time trekking companion Kevin in a backpacker cafe. He was sitting and nursing a hot drink, awake but seemingly in a stupor. His speech was slow, slurred, and sometimes incomprehensible. Rambling, he described how he had already travelled in the direction of Everest Base Camp and returned to Namche. Kevin's lips were chapped and split in places, and his face was dark with severe wind-burn. We parted after making sure Kevin was not about to die from altitude sickness; there was no better place for him to recover. He did not appear to be traveling with any companions. For Kevin, this trek had been a mission, and he didn't look like he had enjoyed it.

On day ten after setting out from Jiri, Jonathan and I hefted our packs to head on towards Gokyo Ri. The trail followed the same Dudh Khosi River valley as before, with the river flowing from north to south. Our final destination would be almost two kilometres higher in altitude. The route gained elevation rapidly over a short distance, and we hoped that travelling for over a week on foot had served to acclimatize us. For this stage, we were joined by three Brits: Padma, Brooke, and Matthew, who were leaving Namche at the same time as us.

The journey would take a few days through yak-grazing lands. We would spend one night at Phortse Tenga and then another at Macchermo before reaching Gokyo village at the base of our destination. The weather was the best yet. The overcast skies at Namche Bazaar gave way to cold but glorious sunshine, with only a few high and wispy cirrus clouds. We were treated to stunning views of snow-capped peaks. Behind us Mount Tramserku towered at 6,608 meters above sea level, framing the picturesque terraced farms at Dole, complete with grazing yaks in the foreground. I finally had a use for my binoculars and caught glimpses of Himalayan thar, a species of wild goat, before a light snow started to fall. We had no yeti sightings.

It was on these final stages of the trail to Gokyo that we made our first wrong turns. The trail crosses and re-crosses the Dudh Khosi River to proceed on the bank that affords the easiest passage by foot. However, the turn-offs to the wooden or steel bridge crossings were not clearly sign-posted. They were easy to miss in the forest. Twice we found our party adding hours to the day, when we were forced to back-track along a river side channel after missing a critical turn. On these mishaps, we had continued head-long through brush, rockslides, and progressively more treacherous terrain until the increasing difficulty of passage made at least one of us realize that we had strayed from the trail. These episodes reinforced the dangers of trekking solo.

At Dole, we were at 4,410 meters in elevation, and Brooke was crying. She retreated a few yards down the hill and sat on a boulder. She gazed out at the magnificent mountain vista, quietly sniffling. Brooke and Matthew had saved for months in London for their dream adventure in Nepal, but now altitude sickness would prevent Brooke from reaching Gokyo Ri only two days away. After sorrowful farewell wishes, Brooke and Matthew turned back towards Phortse Tenga and lower altitudes. Padma continued onwards with Jonathan and me to Machherma.

My own symptoms of altitude sickness appeared to have stabilized. I still had that persistent cough, but unlike Brooke, I didn't experience any nausea or headache. A different and unexpected effect of the altitude was that it increased the frequency I needed to void my bladder at night. I woke up during the night every three hours to pee. I did not much mind these nightly sleep interruptions, however. I always paused on the cold short walk outside, returning from the outhouse to the guesthouse, to stare up at the brilliant Milky Way. The stars were superbly crisp through the thin high-altitude atmosphere.

I thought about a frigid winter night months ago in Calgary, Canada. After leaving home in Toronto, the first part of my journey westward included a few days of skiing at resort towns in the province of Alberta. I was staying with my sister's family in Calgary, and late one night I had gone out to get more firewood from a shed in the yard. Looking up, I saw the Milky Way in a cloudless night sky. The city was gripped in a cold snap of forty degrees below, but I stood transfixed in the freezing darkness as slow-moving satellites among the stars caught my eye. I felt a sense of wonder. I also felt regret that almost three decades had passed before I took the time to look up to watch satellites and shooting stars.

From Machherma, we trekked alongside one of the cloudy brown meltwater streams coming down the west side of the Ngozumpa Glacier. The trail went down, then over a bridge, then climbed to a small lake. We continued upward past a second lake, eventually arriving at the third and largest, the Dudh Pokhari. That third lake was roughly triangular, created from water trapped by the terminal moraine of the glacier, forming a dam across the lower end of the valley. Gokyo Village (4,750 m), our last rest stop before ascending to the final lookout point, consisted of a small group of teahouses next to the frozen lake.

On the morning of the thirteenth day after setting off from Jiri, we awoke to perfect weather in Gokyo. One corner of Dudh Pokhari Lake had thawed. There were a few Brahminy ducks swimming in the vivid turquoise green that is characteristic of glacial lakes. The rest of the lake was a blinding white flatness surrounded by steep mountainsides, littered with loose rock and barren except for lichen. Other than the ducks, the landscape was motionless. The air was completely still, as if the world was holding its breath for our final ascent.

We splurged on a hearty breakfast of eggs and hash browns. Then Padma, Jonathan, and I started in high spirits on the trail up Gokyo Ri. I felt torn between wanting to race upwards to the finish, and wanting to take my time and pause, enjoying the amazing view developing below and around us. We were all slightly short of breath, but the climb was almost easy because we had left our heavy backpacks down in the village guesthouse. None of us felt nausea or dizziness, and I discovered my nagging cough had finally disappeared.

Two hours later, we had walked about 600 meters up and reached the lookout point on Gokyo Ri. A flat stone sign had been set there, carved with the number 5,330. The actual summit of Gokyo Ri is at 5,483 meters but was not easily accessible without technical climbing gear. The lookout was the highest point I would reach in Nepal, roughly the same elevation as the Everest Base Camp from which mountain climbing expeditions start. The day remained windless, and it was unexpectedly warm in the sunshine with a cloud-free deep blue sky. The view was spectacular. Below us, the vast Ngozumpa Glacier, the largest in Nepal, flowed down the Dudh Khosi River Valley in the direction of Namche Bazaar.

From Gokyo Ri, we could see the peaks of four of planet Earth's six highest mountains: to the north was Cho Oyu (8,201 m); to the east were Everest (8,848 m) and Lhotse (8,501 m); and in the distant southeast, we could pick out Makalu (8,463 m). A half dozen peaks seeming almost as high filled the spaces between these giants. We looked down at the endless terminal moraine, and the brilliant turquoise corner of Dudh Pokhari Lake. Looking down at us, even at this extreme elevation, were a couple of ravens, unaffected by the altitude. They flew in circles, dancing amidst the silent, motionless stone giants surrounding us.

We spent three hours on Gokyo Ri, sun tanning, eating a second breakfast of chocolate bars, taking photographs, and drinking rum in the rarified mountain air. Despite the warm weather, Jonathan now pulled out his bright red mittens and asked us to photograph him wearing them on upraised hands. When we asked why, he replied, "Because I bought them in Kathmandu!"

Carl and Jonathan at the Gokyo Ri lookout point, Sagarmatha National Park, Nepal.

10. WE HAVE MOUNTAINS IN OUR CLOUDS

VICTORIOUS AND EXHAUSTED, we retraced our steps from Gokyo south along the valley. Padma and I parted ways with Jonathan before reaching Namche Bazaar. Jonathan decided to turn east towards Pheriche instead. We had heard rumors of a clinic in Pheriche, and Jonathan went to get medical attention for his knees. He also planned to spend a few more days on side treks in this region, if he were physically able. The cold, strain on my own knees, and constant intestinal problems had sapped my energy. I had no appetite for more trekking.

At length, I arrived with Padma back in Lukla. Both of us were planning to board a flight costing seventy-five US dollars on Royal Nepal Airlines back to Kathmandu. Lukla means "place with many goats and sheep," but they must have long since disappeared as trekker food. We trudged over to the airport terminal, which was more like a large shack, where the Asian clerk looked completely discombobulated. He was juggling waiting lists and seemingly random stacks of papers. For over two weeks, the weather had been phenomenal without a drop of rain. However, as is often the case, the clouds had rolled in at Lukla and no planes were taking off or arriving. The twin-engine Otter aircraft serving Lukla carried twenty passengers and were flown by sight. Flying into a cloud in this area could mean you were flying into the side of a mountain. Backlogs of trekkers in Lukla were common, and thousands could be stranded there before the bad weather cleared.

I took my cue from the clouds and chilled. Most trekkers awaiting outbound flights were also patient, resting, eating, and waiting for the fog to dissipate. Everyone splurged on hot-water showers. Teahouse staff heated the water on wood fires that filled the village with smoke and ash. Each year, firewood became scarcer and more expensive, brought in from ever greater distances by porters. But while I enjoyed the extra days of hot showers and recuperation in Lukla, Padma fretted that her travel visa was about to expire. When told that there was no forecast for when the clouds would lift, Padma stoically commented, "Brilliant."

Like me, Padma had a hard time passing herself off as a tourist in Nepal. Except for Cindy, a Japanese-American with whom I had shared a joint in Darjeeling, Padma was the only other non-white backpacker I had met since leaving Canada. She would also be the last, except for an uncommunicative Japanese fellow I would meet months later in Egypt.

Padma had deep set eyes, an aquiline nose, caramel brown skin, and thick straight black hair that she kept in a long braid. She looked as Indian as the large numbers of Indian nationals I'd seen in Kathmandu visiting Nepal on business trips. But Padma had grown up in Manchester and spoke English with a cockney accent.

Padma described how she and her two Caucasian British companions, Brooke and Matthew, had taken a third-class train to travel overnight from Delhi, India to the border with Nepal. In the morning, waking up on the floor of the railcar, there was a decent amount of personal space around Brooke and Matthew and their belongings. Padma, however, opened her eyes to find herself sandwiched by a dozen sleeping local Indians draped over her and her backpack. Apparently, they didn't get the memo that Padma was British too.

Unconsciously, I had adopted Padma's Manchester intonation

when asking questions. Consciously, I teased her that she had forgotten how to finish her words. Instead of "I've got a lot of," she would say, "I've *gaw* a *law ov*." She knitted her brows in thought when I challenged her. Then she proclaimed that clearly enunciating "I've got a lot of" sounded "so *schooo-pid!*"

On our third day in Lukla, the fog did finally lift. A clear view of the Lukla runway did not instill confidence. The runway resembled a narrow gravel lot waiting for a condo development, sloping downwards and ending at a cliff edge. Seeming like a stone's throw from that far edge was the imposing face of the next mountain stretching up into the clouds. It would be a very bumpy take-off, accelerating down the side of one mountain straight towards the side of another. Just after the wheels left the ground, the pilot would need to pull up sharply and turn the plane to avoid catastrophe. It did not help that parts from the wreckage of previous crashed planes had been salvaged and used to mend fences at the far end of the air strip. The flight safety record at Lukla was not good. There had been a lethal plane crash attributed to bad weather about once every two years.

Flights resumed at double or triple the regular frequency to clear the trekker backlog. Padma and I were on the fifth flight out. The baggage check consisted of an airport employee thoroughly massaging the exterior of unopened backpacks before returning them to us to carry over and load onto the plane. This was, of course, ten years before airports the world over would tighten security after the World Trade Towers in New York were destroyed by passenger jets hijacked by terrorists.

Seated inside the small plane to Kathmandu, Padma and I buckled up. Other passengers said prayers. The engines roared, and the bumpy rolling start became a bone-jarring shaky acceleration. We all held our breath, sensing the end was near when the wheels left the ground. The plane swerved to the right, passing a rocky cliff face, blurry through the left side windows. There was a collective and audible exhale from the passengers.

11. MIDNIGHT BASKETBALL

All we ever look for, a god
All we ever look for, ooh, a drug
All we ever look for, a great big hug
All we ever look for, just a little bit of you
All we ever look for, just a little bit of you, too
All we ever look for
But we never do score

"All We Ever Look For"
words and music by Kate Bush

THE FIRST SHOWERS of the rainy season had arrived, and back in warm, wet Kathmandu, the Thamel quarter was subdued. Although the muddy roads were still filled with weaving bicycles, taxis, three-wheelers, motorcycles, and buses, there were fewer beggars in view. Rather than constant harsh cries of "Hallo, hallo!" that would follow you from touts in Indian cities, in Kathmandu you heard furtive whispers of "Change money?" "Shoe shine?" or "*Ganja?*" *Ganja* is the Sanskrit word for the dried buds of the marijuana plant.

The penalty for possession of drugs in Nepal was severe. If you were caught by a policeman smoking ganja, you would merely be taken down to the station to bribe your way to freedom. But being caught with heroin, cocaine, or amphetamines meant jail time. In Kathmandu, I met Adele while she was putting up posters at the various backpacker haunts. The posters encouraged travelers to visit hapless backpackers who were serving lengthy jail sentences in Kathmandu for drug offences.

Adele was an Irish girl of no fixed address. She was an individual of a species of "resident backpacker" that spent several months living in one Asian city before moving on to the next. For now, Adele was working at a Kathmandu café while continuing her studies of meditation and music. Though she was willowy and slender, I found her somehow larger than life. I was enchanted by her emerald green eyes, airy self-confidence, and individuality. I spent hours at that café, chatting with Adele about spirituality, religion, and the purpose of our lives. Perhaps unsurprisingly, Adele was transitioning herself from the Christian Catholic faith, into which she had been born, towards Buddhism instead.

Buddhism is everywhere in Kathmandu. Just take a walk in Durbar Square, always bustling with the morning market, pungent with carrots, peas, cucumbers, oranges, apples, radishes, bananas, tubers, and all manner of leafy green stuff. The people are varied, and you see tiny wrinkled old women selling fresh produce, porters trudging under impossible loads, brisk Asian businessmen working at computers behind windows, and smiling pleasant Nepali shopkeepers. But standing out from everyone else are the shaven heads of Buddhist monks wearing orange and rust-red robes, walking to or from one of the many temples in the square.

In contrast to the multi-tiered and extravagant *gopurhams* of Hindu temples, covered with dozens of carved deity figures, Nepalese temples are relatively austere shrines to the Buddha. Buddhist shrines are not places to ask favours of, worship, or seek guidance from God or gods. Instead, Buddhists go to their temples to practice the teachings of a human, Siddhartha Guatama. This man, Gautama, lived in ancient East India and Nepal between the sixth and fourth-century BCE. Gautama was able to achieve a state of enlightenment, or *nirvana*. Nirvana is described as a state of peace, joy, understanding of the universe, and the end to the suffering of life. Buddhist individuals and monks follow the guidance of the Buddha to break an endless cycle of life, death, and reincarnation by achieving nirvana. Buddhists seek nirvana through acting with compassion for all things, meditation, and personal development.

Buddhist temples, or *stupas*, are large white domes with an entrance, topped with a golden spire. At the base of the spire above the dome sits a square block with large painted eyes on its four vertical sides. These Buddha Eyes, or Wisdom Eyes, look to the north, south, east, and west, and symbolize the omniscience of a Buddha. Between the eyes is what looks like a stylized nose but is actually the Nepali character for the number one, symbolizing that unity with all things is a way to reach nirvana. Inside, the stupa houses a relic, which is either a significant object once owned by an important monk, or part of his cremated body.

Three kilometres west of the Thamel Quarter, I climbed the steps of a small hill to the Buddhist Swayambhunath Temple. This stupa is also known as the Monkey Temple because of the monkeys living in the northwest corner of the temple grounds. Legend has it that these are holy monkeys, transformed from lice (weird!) that lived on the head of the monk Manjushri. According to legend, Kathmandu was originally covered by a lake, with a lotus plant floating in the centre of the water. Manjushri drained the lake by magic and transformed the lotus plant into the hill on which Swayambhunath temple was built.

There were no monks around Swayambhunath at the time of my visit. I walked slowly around the perimeter of the white cement dome, spinning the cylindrical prayer wheels set in a wrought iron fence that encircled the stupa's base. Outside, I pretended to be a spiritual person. Inside, I was an awkward imposter miming a religious ritual. I spun the wheels so that the believers would not challenge me. It was the same feeling I had felt as a kindergartener, when my mother took me to a Christian Presbyterian church service in Toronto. *What are all these religious people feeling that I don't? Do they hear God's voice in their heads? What is 'praying'? Why don't they just work for what they want, instead of asking God to give it for free?* I had been much too shy as a child to ask any of these questions out loud.

Back at the Kathmandu guesthouse, I settled in, vomited up lunch, and then went to hang out in the common area. When I entered, it was occupied by a tall blond Australian fellow. Robert was almost six feet tall and in his early twenties. He didn't have much of an Aussie accent, having spent a few years in the United States. He was preparing himself a snack, spreading Vegemite on toast. Eager to perpetuate the Aussie stereotype, he was happy to extoll the superiority of Vegemite over Marmite, that *other* brand of yeast-extract condiment favored by the citizens of Britain. Robert had an easy, self-confident manner and a penchant for mischief.

Later, I had dinner with Robert at Narula's, the popular Indian fast-food chain famous for its slogan of offering twenty-one flavors of ice cream. When we arrived back at the hostel, the buzz amongst the travelers was about a gambling excursion. For a small fare, a bus would shuttle us to Casino Nepal in the five-star Annapurna Hotel, and then back to the Thamel area at the end of the evening. Several other luxury hotels in the city also had casinos, including the Crowne Plaza, Yak & Yeti, and the Everest Hotel in Kathmandu.

The exchange rate at the time was about thirty Nepalese rupees to the Canadian dollar. More important was the purchasing power parity. While in 1991 you could buy a bottle of Coca-Cola for about fifty cents in Canada, that same bottle of Coke would cost you only five rupees in Nepal, or about fifteen cents. The minimum bet in the Nepali casino was two rupees, or six Canadian cents. This was my chance to be a high-roller!

When the bus pulled up, the casino was nothing like flashy North American clubs. Although it was a decent hotel, the Annapurna had no extravagant Vegas-style fountains, miniaturized Eiffel Towers, or bright advertisements featuring semi-nude young ladies. It was just a hotel, with a door in the lobby leading to the gambling rooms. Of course, I was hassled at that door. Nepali law forbids gambling by Nepali citizens; only foreigners were permitted to gamble. The passengers on the shuttle bus included a few western tourists, but the majority were Indian nationals on business trips. It took Caucasian Robert and other backpackers to vouch for me that my Canadian passport was not a fake, and that I was not a Nepali trying to skirt the law.

We filed inside the doorway and entered the low murmuring of maybe a hundred gamblers in inter-connected rooms. Each room offered a different game. Entrance to the casino was free, but everyone was required to buy a minimum amount in chips. Robert and I went to the cashier to get tokens for the slot machines.

Unfortunately, not only had I never visited a casino in North America before, I was also not familiar with any casino card games except blackjack, or "Twenty-One." I had heard that even that simple game had specific rules of etiquette for whether to accept another card from the casino dealer or to "stand" with the cards already in my hand. If you didn't follow the rules, you messed it up for the next person around the table when it was his or her turn with the dealer. Afraid of looking stupid at cards, or offending other players, I contented myself with the slot machines and put a few chips on the roulette wheel, slowly dispensing the 200 rupees in tokens I had budgeted for the evening.

Robert, however, was a side-splitting Aussie clown all night. He was a high-stakes poker player with phenomenal luck. It helped that he didn't care if he lost a bluff, because it was impossible for him to lose serious money. I don't think he folded even once against the comparatively cash-strapped Indian players at his table. In the end, after many wins and losses, he came away with a healthy gain of about a hundred rupees, or just over three dollars in Canadian currency.

After a few hours of pulling handles at the slot machines, watching spinning images of mismatched fruit, I'd had enough. On my third Fanta, I persuaded Robert that it was time to go. There was a twenty-minute wait for the shuttle, and then we departed for our guesthouse.

But we hit a snag. Instead of dropping us near our guesthouse or at any familiar landmark in Thamel, the shuttle bus unexpectedly stopped in a wide, deserted plaza in the middle of the night. The driver switched the engine off. No doubt the Indian passengers all recognized their whereabouts; silently, they filed off the bus and scattered like rats into the darkness. Before we realized it, the bus driver had also disappeared. Robert and I were completely baffled and lost standing next to the empty parked bus.

"Any clue which way?" I asked.

"I think ... that way?" Robert gestured vaguely in his suggested direction. "I haven't been to this place before either," he added.

"Okay," I agreed. "Let's head that way and see if we can find someone to give us directions."

Kathmandu's old town in the area around Durbar Square is a maze of streets, alleys, and courtyards, and empty at that hour. Most streets in old Kathmandu are not straight, and some have interesting S-curves. Many of the streets are lined on both sides by continuous high stone walls. There are doors and windows in these walls for the individual homes behind. We also passed metal shutters over garage-door-sized openings that would reveal shops and businesses during the day.

Regardless of the hour, Kathmandu feels very safe. Neither of us was the least bit nervous as we passed the darkened doorways and shadowy openings. And then we heard the sounds of a bouncing ball and shuffling feet. Rounding yet another corner, we came upon another wide plaza dimly lit by electric streetlights, and we were saved by a pick-up basketball game at one a.m. in the morning.

With brazen self-confidence, Robert asked if we could join the game. He playfully dubbed us the "Hot-Shot Trekkers" while naming the other team the "Local Boys."

We played two on three. It was not the easiest thing to play basketball wearing hiking boots. But the Hot-Shot Trekkers had the clear advantage in height. Robert's height, that is. While I was one or two inches taller than the Local Boys, my companion towered over them. I hadn't played basketball since eighth grade in public school. I didn't have shot accuracy either, but I could at least dribble and pass. For about twenty minutes, I blocked, dribbled, and fed the ball to Robert, who would deftly waltz in for a lay-up, or simply stand with the ball held high over his head and shoot for the basket. With every basket for us or the Local Boys, Robert would cheerfully call out the score in a running monologue.

The Local Boys didn't seem overly happy to be on the losing end. However, they were gracious enough to help us find our hostel afterwards. One of them recognized the name of the street for our guesthouse and led us through the night, turning a series of lefts and rights. We had been totally lost. Robert and I were relieved when, at length, we emerged near our hotel. It was another testament to the ability of clueless backpackers to muddle through any challenge.

12. HIGH IN VARANASI

FROM KATHMANDU I travelled to Pokhara on another sun-drenched but dusty eight-hour roof-top bus ride. On the following day, the weather gods deserted me, and the pre-monsoon rains came. I had come to Pokhara to see picturesque Phewa Lake framed by the Annapurna peaks. During the two days of my stay, however, the idyllic tourist hamlet was completely smothered by cloud, rain, and drizzle. Disappointed, I tried to enjoy the cool humidity, nonetheless. I splurged at several of the town's restaurants.

On the third day, I acquiesced and let the rain clouds take their turn. I headed south back to India. The trip did not start well. I had a heated argument with the Nepali driver of the bus. He, too, was convinced I was a Nepali citizen, and refused to recognize my Canadian passport. All the other bus passengers were Indian nationals crossing the border. In the end, the driver allowed me to board the bus but made me sit in an aisle space between seats at the back. Was this reverse racism?

At length, I arrived in Varanasi on May 8, 1991. As it is written in travel guides, Varanasi is the India of your imagination. Its old town ranks as the most labyrinthine I have ever had the pleasure of wandering. Following my usual habit, I went out on a walking exploration in the evening. The city was alive with markets and open-fronted shops. I wandered happily. The market wares were illuminated by warm yellow light from tungsten bulbs, or the garish green glow of fluorescent tubes. There were shops selling hand-beaten copper and brass platters and bowls. There were showrooms of elaborate silk and gold brocade *saris*. Other stores displayed a lifetime's supply of jewelry boxes, ashtrays, and candle holders. There were shelves crowded with trinkets made from clay, ivory, and carved stone. You could buy carpets and musical instruments.

When I'd had enough, I turned back towards the guesthouse. After walking for half an hour searching for a familiar street or landmark, however, I realized I was hopelessly lost in the twisting streets. Passersby and shopkeepers either didn't recognize the name of my hotel or did not speak enough English to help me. Finally, I found a teenager who spoke passable English who assured me he knew the way. I thought perhaps he would lead me for five minutes and turn a corner to a street I would recognize, but instead he led me at a brisk pace for over twenty minutes before I was able to pick out a familiar building. I would never have found my way back that night on my own. The boy had not named a price in advance but was happy when I handed him a ten-rupee note.

The city of Varanasi is bordered on the southeast by the curving bank of the Ganges River. At many places along the riverbank are generously wide stone steps leading right down into the water. Each set of steps is known as a *ghat*. There are about ninety Varanasi ghats, mostly built during the 1700s by rulers of the Maratha Empire. Today, you can go down to the ghats to see men bathing in the polluted water; women standing in the river beating clothes against wooden washboards; herds of cows going down for a drink; or worshippers performing *puja*, Hindu prayers.

Darbhanga Ghat in Varanasi, India.

There are a few special ghats for cremating bodies. Every Hindu aspires to have his body cleansed after death by the holy waters of the Ganges at these burning ghats. After being dunked in the river, or drenched with Ganges water from pails, the soggy body is burnt on a huge pile of firewood waiting on the ghat. When the fire is done, the ashes are scattered into the river while the soul flies upward to heaven. Small forests are consumed to support up to eighty cremations a day. Rich people import expensive wood like sandalwood or teak for their funeral pyres. Everyone is worried about the pollution from smoke and ashes, but the burning does not slow. Overnight, I could usually spot one or two corpses wrapped in white fabric like mummies, waiting to be set on fire the following day. Stray dogs barked as they tried to gnaw on the dead but were kicked away by hired guards.

It was in Varanasi that I encountered the government *bhang* shops, essentially selling legalized hashish. *Bhang*, similar to hash or hashish, is an edible paste made from grinding the buds and leaves of the marijuana plant. Indians have been adding bhang to their food and drink for at least 3,000 years. The drug is used to relax, achieve transcendental states while meditating, and celebrate Hindu festivals such as *Diwali*, the festival of light in December. Legend says that Shiva, the lord of bhang, brought it from the Himalayas as a gift for mankind. It seems this Shiva is a likeable fellow. Bhang is such an inextricable element in Indian culture and religion that the modern-day Indian government cannot make it illegal, as it is in Canada and the US. Instead, bhang is a regulated substance in India, like tobacco and alcohol. Hence, the government bhang shops, selling hash cookies.

I could not resist the temptation of buying a cookie.

The bhang cookies appeared to be made of sesame seed paste, hashish, and some kind of flour. The sign reading "Government Bhang Shop" outside was hand-painted. Still skeptical that it was legal, I bought only one cookie and discreetly hid it in my pocket before leaving the shop. Years later, I learned that bhang from these shops is strictly reserved for Hindu ceremonial use. Foreign travelers who purchased bhang could be thrown in jail for possession of drugs. The shopkeeper, however, had shown no qualms about taking my cash.

Back at the hostel, I tentatively ate a third of the cookie. I was expecting to feel a pleasant narcotic high, but I had read that too much hash would cause delirium, hallucinations, and nausea. It tasted like a soft gingerbread cookie. Nothing. I finished the cookie and felt not the slightest effect from the bhang. I concluded that it must be like smoking a joint, with no discernable effect until you consumed enough of the drug to saturate your system.

The next day, I bought two more bhang cookies from the same shop, and ate them for desert in my room after returning from a dinner out. Again, I did not experience any drug effect at all, but they were pretty good-tasting cookies. I munched away, while reading a used copy of *The Satanic Verses* by Salman Rushdie that I had found in Pokhara. An hour later, Heather knocked at my door.

I'd met Heather the day before. I had just bought three iridescent silk brocade wall hangings from the market and was showing them off to the concierge in the lobby. Heather was staying at the same hotel, and the shiny silks caught her eye as she came in from the street. We started talking about the Indian tradition of shopkeepers inviting passersby into their shops for some complimentary tea. Once seated inside, there is the inevitable sales pitch where you are treated like royalty being presented exquisite gifts laid out before you as tribute. Heather and I bonded instantly. We went out to a dinner of Kashmiri *pilau*, and then ended the night with an amazing free sitar concert in a community hall.

Now, I let Heather into my room, grabbing hold of the door frame to steady myself. Unfortunately, I discovered her speech had become way too fast for me to understand. I began to feel disturbingly heavy, weak, and physically helpless.

The room was small and spartan. Heather kicked off her sandals and sat cross-legged at one end of the bed, wearing a t-shirt and shorts. While Heather was talking, time was stretching, and then speeding up again. I kept looking at my watch, vainly trying to keep track of the true passage of time.

"It takes all kinds to make a world," said Heather, in her sultry voice.

For the life of me, I couldn't remember what we were just talking about or why she had made that comment. "Uh, yeah, I guess you're right," I said. I was keenly aware that we were now both sitting on my bed. I was torn between wanting her to stay and wanting her to leave, so I could just put my head down and close my eyes.

"Do you think there is any place open for chocolate?" she asked.

"Um, sure," I replied, having not a clue. I tried to paste a confident expression on my face.

"Really? It's kind of late. Where do think we should go?" she asked. She looked at me with those incredibly large soft brown eyes. She had a slightly pouty mouth.

"You know what? I had a couple of those hash cookies sold by the government shops, and I think they remembered to add the hash to them this time. I am high as a kite, not making any sense, but I'd love to meet up with you in the morning," I apologized.

Actually, I was far too immature and lacking in self-confidence to say this. What I really said was, "Uh ... I think we could just head out and look for a place." With each passing minute, it was increasingly difficult to speak without slurring my words.

Eventually, Heather either realized I was a drugged-up idiot or decided that wandering the streets looking for a café still open at that hour was a fool's errand. We agreed to meet early the next morning for breakfast, and to go down to a nearby ghat to charter a boat tour on the Ganges.

After that, I drifted in and out of sleep while in my head I watched psychedelic videos. These were just like the pop-music videos popular at the time on Music TV. Rainbows and kaleidoscopic pinwheels swirled before my eyes, as animated caricatures of the Beatles, Einstein, and Dido performed acrobatics. I didn't wake up for sixteen hours.

13. IN WITH THE ISRAELIS

EAST OF VARANASI lies Khajuraho, the forgotten city of erotic temples. Another UNESCO World Heritage site, these stone temples were built between 950 and 1050 CE and are covered with elaborate carvings of creative and challenging sex positions. They are definitive proof that Hinduism is a fun religion. I came away with a new understanding that no sex act, no matter how unusual, physically unlikely, or perverted, has not already been tried during our 200,000-year history as *Homo sapiens*.

From Khajuraho, I treated myself to an air-conditioned first-class express train to Agra. On the train, I fell in with Sefi and his Israeli backpacker clique. Sefi explained that lots of Israeli young people backpacked through India, and the Sinai in Egypt, because border restrictions in many other countries barred Israeli citizens from entry at the time. I learned that, with the Israelis, you were either "in" their circle or "out." And once you were in, you were *all* in.

When we arrived at the Agra train station on the outskirts of town, we were met by almost a dozen rickshaw drivers shouting a barrage of "Hallo, hallo!" Methodically, the Israelis split themselves up into three groups and commenced the bargaining ritual. Each group dickered with a different subset of Indian drivers, asking about the fare, whether the fare was per passenger, and how long it would take to get to the destination neighbourhood.

Without making any commitments, the Israelis then signaled each other and coalesced into one group to consult in Hebrew. In short order, the Israelis agreed on the driver with the winning bid. Switching back to English, Sefi asked in a loud voice which of the other rickshaw drivers would match the deal. Three more drivers accepted. Then the entire Israeli group, including me, loaded up, two backpackers per vehicle.

As we entered the guesthouse neighbourhood of Agra, everyone dumped their packs in a heap at the side of the road. Sefi and I guarded our belongings while the other Israelis scattered to scout options to accommodate the entire group. They pre-arranged a time and place to meet after twenty minutes of reconnaissance. Again, the best option for the group was determined, and an acceptable establishment was located with enough rooms to shelter all eight of us.

We were all on one floor in the guesthouse. Every day, I could hear the Israelis calling to each other across the halls, through the open doors of their individual rooms. Interestingly, much of the Israeli banter was in English. Who had soap? Who had an extra padlock? What time should everyone meet for dinner? How many needed laundry services? Every Israeli's needs were looked after; no one was left out of the group. Sefi explained that this is essentially survival behavior developed from decades of living with the Arab threat at home. The eyes and ears of every Israeli citizen constantly scanned for Palestinian suicide bombers or gunmen, ready to sound the alarm. No Israeli was left to fend for him or herself.

In the streets of Agra, Indian touts would single me out as I wandered in the company of the Israeli clique. For once not trying to sell me something, they would quietly ask, "Why are you traveling with such a disagreeable people?" Sefi and the gang were continuously engaged in vigorous haggling. The Israelis seemed to delight in grinding-down obviously destitute Indians, well beyond the degree to which I felt comfortable as a visitor from wealthy

Canada. Candidly acknowledging this with a sheepish smile, Sefi the Israeli traveler said, "Israeli travelers are not nice."

Yes, the Israelis were loud. To a native English speaker, their tone often sounded rude, even in everyday casual remarks to each other. They were unfailingly aggressive in money matters and did not mingle either with Indian locals or other international backpackers. I had many conversations with Sefi, comparing life in Israel to Canada. The prevalence (or lack) of guns in civilian society. Compulsory military service for Israeli youth, while most Canadian high school grads shied away from military careers because of pacifist leanings. Endless debating between Orthodox Jews and liberal Jews in Israel, while in Canada fewer and fewer people even bothered to go to church. The fact that the Canadian passport was welcomed the world over, while only a few countries would admit Israeli tourists at the time. I never understood why Sefi's group adopted me, but I was grateful for my time with them.

One does not visit Agra without a visit to the Taj Mahal. The Taj was built in 1643 by Muslim Emperor Shah Jahan as the tomb for his favourite wife, Mumtaz Mahal. She died while giving birth to their fourteenth child (holy crap!). It was a time in history when one ruler could still pay for the work of 20,000 craftsmen or commoners, and it took sixteen years to build the Taj.

You enter the gardens in front of the Taj through the Great Gate, a red sandstone structure. The Arabic on the Great Gate reads *"O Soul, thou art at rest. Return to the Lord at peace with Him, and He at peace with you."* This verse is written with black marble pieces, precisely cut and embedded flush with the white marble panel on the gate wall. The Arabic characters grow progressively larger with elevation, so that to a reader at ground level all the writing appears to be the same size from bottom to top.

In front of the mausoleum itself, there is a long shallow rectangular pool dividing the gardens, to create the famous aqueous mirror image of the white building. The pool was dry and filled with grass during my visit, but the sunny weather compensated for any disappointment. The interior of the tomb itself dazzles with semi-precious stone inlay. Photography was not allowed inside. Consistent with the Muslim faith, there are no depictions of living things, and all the decorations are either calligraphy (verses from the Quran) or abstract shapes and patterns.

I felt vaguely let down. The Taj was a detached and unmoving experience. Nothing in that magnificent building gave me any impression of the woman entombed within, a human being who was once loved and mourned.

14. NIGHT OF THE ASSASSINATION

IT WAS EARLY EVENING and I was in a taxi *en route* to the Delhi train station. I relaxed in the back seat with my pack beside me as we sped through the city streets. My train to Amritsar was due to arrive at the station around eight o'clock.

For the past few weeks, Indians had been preparing to open the gates of unreason in the name of democracy. For the 1991 general elections, the main parties included the Hindu nationalist Bharatiya Janata Party (whose slogan was *India for Hindus!*), the secular Indian National Congress, and many other parties running on platforms of communism, the Muslim religion, minority-caste empowerment, and so forth. Periodically, soldiers blockaded the Delhi streets for the incumbent Prime Minister's motorcade. The city seemed to be holding its breath in anticipation of election violence. It seemed every dawn brought the expectation of news about another political assassination in the state of Punjab. The Punjab had a history of seeking independence for its largely Sikh population using tactics that involved killing.

I felt it was a very long ride to Delhi Junction, but for backpacker travel you need to have faith that the cab driver will get you to your destination. The cabbie made a number of turns, and then I had no idea what part of the city was passing.

I arrived at a large train station that was not too busy. I crisscrossed it several times before finding the platform number of my train, printed on the ticket I'd purchased from a travel agent a few days before. While I waited, the station loudspeakers came alive periodically to make announcements in Hindi. They were quite loud but utterly unintelligible to me. I could not even be certain whether the announcements were in Hindi or heavily accented English. Maybe "Hindlish"?

At the appointed hour, my train to Amritsar did not show. I gave it a few more minutes, and then proceeded to inquire at the ticket windows, perplexed. There were two that were still occupied. I picked one, and I asked the fellow inside. He informed me in passable English that the train had broken down halfway out of its last stop before reaching Delhi. Didn't I hear the announcements?

No one knew how long repairs would take or when the delayed train would eventually arrive at Delhi station. There was no option but to sit and wait. By nine or ten o'clock, there were few people remaining at the station except for several beggars. Each beggar was trying to become as inconspicuous as possible in a dim corner to pass the night. There was a large waiting room on the second floor, with some plastic chairs and a few tables. I found an unoccupied seat to wait out the hours and doze until my train pulled in. The night was cool, and the beggars in the room covered themselves up with shawls.

I was half asleep when two policemen entered the room. One had a long thin stick, which he used to tap the floor in front of him to announce his approach as he walked. In a loud voice, he roused the beggars and told them to move on. I watched as these officers proceeded systematically to eject beggars from the waiting room, eventually reaching my chair. I was asked for my travel documents and where I was headed. I wondered if this train-station patrol was a routine clearing of the beggars. However, I wanted my interaction with Indian police to be as brief and trouble-free as possible. I didn't ask any questions.

Satisfied with my documents, the police officers left me and continued evicting beggars from the room. An hour after the officers had come and gone, every single one of those beggars had returned. By two a.m., I was exhausted from lack of sleep and despairing that the train would ever arrive. I returned downstairs and found that the ticket seller to whom I had spoken earlier was still on duty. I asked for an update.

The ticket seller advised me that my best bet at that point was to catch a different train for Amritsar, leaving at seven a.m. the next morning. However, I had to catch that train from another train station. "You are at Delhi Junction," he said. "You are at *old* Delhi Railway Station. Train to Amritsar leaves from *Nooo* Delhi Railway Station."

Brilliant. I went to another service booth and got a refund for my ticket on the broken-down train. Now, I needed to hail another cab and take a twenty-minute ride back in the direction of the hotel I had checked out from near Connaught Place in downtown New Delhi. As there were still many hours before the other train was due to depart, I was annoyed at the inconvenience and extra taxi cost but not worried.

In a cab again, I closed my eyes, tired from the sleepless night. We sped through the deserted streets in the dark. Suddenly there were flashes of light, a siren, and a police car forcing the taxi to pull over. Three policemen stepped out of the cruiser, and one of them jabbered at the cab driver in Hindi, shining a flashlight in his face and inspecting his license and taxi permits. Then the officer turned to me, shining his light to illuminate the back seats.

"Can you step out, please," the officer instructed politely. I got out, wondering what was about to happen.

For the second time that night, a policeman asked for my passport, and then my train ticket.

"For what reason do you go to Amritsar?" was the next question.

"Just tourism. I want to visit the Golden Temple," I answered. Tentatively, I added, "What's going on?"

The policeman ignored my question but seemed satisfied with my documents. The other officers had by this time fished out my backpack, placed it on the hood of the taxi, poked at it, and then quickly pawed through the contents. They found nothing suspicious. I wondered if I would be hit up for a bribe.

His face giving away nothing, the officer with my documents handed them back. "Have a good holiday," he said, and turned away. My backpack was zipped up and passed back to me.

Puzzled, I settled again into the rear of the cab as the police drove away. *Probably just a random security check,* I thought. The cab driver shook his head, saying he did not know anything more than I did. He started the cab's engine, and we continued on our way. After a few more minutes, I found myself at the New Delhi Railway Station. I paid the cabbie his fare with a tip, shouldering my pack. My train finally pulled in at six o'clock in the morning. I boarded after the passengers arriving at Delhi had cleared the platform.

It was May 22, 1991, and I discovered why New Delhi security forces had been on high alert the night before. The newspaper headlines revealed that yesterday, Rajiv Gandhi, former Prime Minister of India, had been assassinated by a suicide bomber.

With the imminent election, tensions had already been high between Hindu and Sikh citizens of the country. Rajiv was a Hindu, leading the Indian National Congress Party. Rajiv's mother was Indira Gandhi, who had been the third Prime Minister of India until she was assassinated by Sikhs in 1984. During that earlier time of political unrest, Indira had ordered the Indian army to force its way into the Golden Temple at Amritsar and extract a militant religious leader, Jarnail Singh Bhindranwale. The Golden Temple happens to be the holiest place of worship for Sikhs. The temple was heavily damaged during the assault. A few months later, Indira was gunned down by two of her own bodyguards, who were Sikhs taking revenge for the desecration of their temple.

Immediately after Rajiv's death, no one knew who was responsible. The Sikhs were being treated with suspicion. And this morning, I had just arrived at Amritsar. Perfect timing.

As it turned out, the suicide bomber who killed Rajiv was a Tamil woman. Sikhs had nothing to do with the latest assassination. Rajiv Gandhi was running for re-election after losing office two years before. During an interview, he had said that, if re-elected, he would send the Indian army to Sri Lanka to neutralize the Tamil Tiger fighters there. Sri Lanka is an island country just off India's south coast. Sri Lanka was in the middle of a nasty civil war between the mostly Sinhalese population and the Tamil population in the northern part of the island who wanted an independent state.

Many Tamil people living in India were not happy about Rajiv's plans for their Tamil relatives in Sri Lanka. Rajiv was campaigning in Chennai, in the Indian state of Tamil Nadu. A woman at the political rally, Thenmozhi Rajaratnam, pretended she was a supporter of Rajiv. She approached him before he gave his speech and placed a garland of flowers around Rajiv's neck. Then she reached down and detonated an explosive belt hidden under her skirt. The blast killed Rajiv, Thenmozhi, and twelve other people. We know all this because it was captured on camera by one of the men killed in the blast.

I discovered that Amritsar was the most peaceful, quiet, clean, and relaxed Indian city I had visited so far. There were hardly any beggars and few touts. After settling into a guesthouse, I went to visit the Golden Temple. The temple sits in the middle of a man-made pool or tank, creating the illusion that the building is afloat. You reach the temple by walking barefoot along a paved narrow causeway.

The Golden Temple of Amritsar is in Punjab state, home to India's population of Sikhs. After Taoism, Hinduism and Buddhism, Sikhism was the fourth major world religion I encountered on my journey (or fifth if you included Christianity). The Sikh religion began only 500 years ago, founded by Guru Nanak born in 1469. Like Jesus, Guru Nanak preached a message of love. Nanak criticized the religious rituals of the Hindus and Muslims around him. He thought rituals like fasting or pilgrimage were pointless. He did not believe in worshipping dead people or objects that represented gods or God. Like Christians and Jews, Guru Nanak preached that there is only one God. Sikhs believe that men, women, and people of different races and religions are all equal in the eyes of God.

Guru Nanak was succeeded by nine more Gurus, all men. The tenth Guru, Guru Gobind Singh, came to the conclusion that by his time in power, the Sikh priests had all become corrupt and preoccupied with increasing their own wealth and influence. And so, Guru Singh abolished the entire Sikh priesthood. Sikhs do not believe you need to isolate yourself as a priest, monk, or nun to become closer to God.

In an even more unusual move, in 1708 before he died, Guru Gobind Singh instructed his followers to treat the Sikh holy book, the Guru Granth Sahib, as the eleventh Guru. Just as some now fear that humans will eventually be replaced with artificial intelligence and robots, there will be no more human Gurus after they were replaced by a book. The book sets out the Code of Conduct and Conventions that Sikhs follow to merge or re-unite with God in perfect happiness. Sikhs work towards this goal by meditating, performing selfless service, avoiding drugs and alcohol, fighting injustice, and being faithful to their spouses. The Guru Granth

Sahib also requires Sikh men to wear a turban and carry a *Kirpan*, a small ceremonial sword.

The Golden Temple is in fact coated with about 750 kilograms of gold. Every morning, the Guru Granth Sahib is placed inside the temple, and every evening the holy book is returned to the Akal Takhat (Timeless Throne) building on the perimeter of the pool at the entrance to the causeway. These days, there is an endless stream of Sikh pilgrims awaiting their turn at the causeway. In 1991 when I visited, there were only a handful of worshippers in line and no tourists except for me. Attendants loaned me a scarf to wrap around my head as I took off my shoes. I walked the fifty-meter path across the water to the temple. Inside the temple, I saw Guru Granth Sahib, but I don't remember what it looked like. The book is written in Gurmukhi, a form of the ancient Sanskrit language, and no photography was allowed.

Before visiting Amritsar, I knew almost nothing about the Sikh religion, but I had a vague impression that its followers were prone to violence. At home in Canada, I had read news stories about the Sikh nationalist Khalistan movement. Sikh separatists were using terrorism to try to create an independent state called Khalistan in the Punjab region of India. A Canadian politician, Ujjal Dosanjh, spoke out against Sikhs using violence to achieve political objectives. Then he was beaten up by a Sikh with a steel pipe. Canadian Sikh extremists were responsible for the 1985 Air India bombing, killing 329 mostly Hindu people flying from Montreal to Delhi. The bombing remains the largest mass killing in Canadian history.

By contrast, the people I met in Amritsar were quiet, gentle, and sociable middle-aged men in turbans. Here they were all gathering at the Jallianwala Bagh Courtyard. The public courtyard is enclosed by high walls on all four sides, with only one narrow lane to get in and out. In a strange twist, this group of men was gathering peacefully at the site of a massacre. In 1919, a crowd of Indians had converged there to support Mahatma Gandhi's non-violent protest against their country's occupation by Britain. British Colonel Reginald Dyer ordered his soldiers to open fire on the unarmed Indian protesters. Somewhere between 400 to 1,000 people were shot to death, including women and children, trapped by the courtyard walls.

You can still see the bullet holes in the brick walls today. Nearing the hundredth anniversary of the 1919 massacre, Indian politicians are pressing the British government for an official apology.

I watched as Sikh men filed into the courtyard and sat cross-legged on the grass in small groups. The conversation was subdued and quiet. I did not know whether this lunch-time crowd was a regular gathering, but the men were talking about the previous day's assassination of Rajiv Gandhi. They all shook their heads, sadly condemning the violence. Curiously, two separate groups of these men spotted the camera in my hands and asked me to take their photographs. In that pre-internet age, there was no easy means for me to send the pictures I took with my 35mm film camera back to them in Amritsar, India, after developing the prints in Canada.

One elderly Sikh man gently took my arm to get my attention. With a solemn expression, he sadly pointed out a well where some of the Indian protesters in 1919 had jumped to escape the British gunfire. The Guru Granth Sahib instructs its Sikh followers to "fight injustice." It seemed a curious contradiction of Sikhs who condemned violence using it in their struggle for a separate homeland.

15. THE SATANIC VERSES IN AMRITSAR

NO DOUBT MANY WILL question the wisdom of my choice, but in order to learn a bit about the Muslim faith before entering Pakistan, I was reading *The Satanic Verses*. This novel by Salman Rushdie was first published in 1988. The book is a fictional story about two men who magically survive an explosion in a hijacked airplane. In one minor sub-plot of the story, Rushdie retells, but changes, the early history of Islam. Islam is the religion that began with the Prophet Muhammad, and people who follow Islam call themselves Muslims. In Rushdie's imaginary version of the beginning of Islam, the prophet Muhammad receives the pages of the Muslim holy book, the Quran, but the pages are mixed up and contain changes introduced by the Devil. Because of this mischief, modern Muslims following the guidance of the sabotaged Quran are doomed to insanity and rituals that make no sense.

Despite being obviously a work of fiction, Muslims worldwide were outraged. They sent death threats to Rushdie. Right after the book was published, there was a violent riot against it in Pakistan. Pakistan and other predominantly Muslim countries banned the novel. The supreme leader of Iran, the Ayatollah Khomeini, issued an order calling for every Muslim in the world to assassinate Rushdie. The Japanese and Italian translators of the novel were both stabbed. The Norwegian publisher was shot. Bookstores selling the novel in the United States were bombed. *The Satanic Verses* created a conflict between western democracies supporting freedom of expression and Muslim nations forbidding anyone from criticizing Muhammad. British Prime Minister Margaret Thatcher was forced to provide round-the-clock police protection to Rushdie, who by 1991 had been living in hiding in London for three years.

I took a taxi from Amritsar thirty kilometres west to Attari, the Indian border town. Now, about to cross into the Islamic Republic of Pakistan, I belatedly realized it might not be the best idea to have *The Satanic Verses* in my baggage. Ironically, I didn't know at the time that the book had also been banned in India. Although it was not a crime to own or read it, Indian law prohibited the book from being imported, which I had unwittingly done by bringing the used paperback with me on the bus from Pokhara, Nepal. Blissfully ignorant, I wanted to finish the few pages I had remaining at the end of the story, just before I crossed the border into Pakistan.

Afraid of being caught with a banned item by customs officers of an authoritarian state, I did what any traveler in my position would: I went to the washroom. Entering the border control building on the India side, I went to the men's washroom with the novel hidden in my small day pack. The washroom was empty, with three western-style toilet stalls along one wall, spotlessly clean and odour-free. Great. I took a seat on a porcelain throne, closed the door, and began to read.

It was a satisfying conclusion. When I'd finished, twenty minutes later, I placed *The Satanic Verses* discreetly behind the white ceramic bowl for a janitor to discover.

From Attari, I cleared customs and walked across to Wahga on the Pakistani side without incident. Since the time of my visit, tension between India and Pakistan has escalated. I think the number of travelers crossing at Attari-Wahga has dropped off. However, back in 1991, I was greeted on the Wahga side by touts cheerfully selling trinkets in the bright afternoon sun.

Many of the souvenirs had a slogan for tourists, just like "I love New York," "Ontario, yours to discover," or "It's better in the Bahamas." Pakistan had a clear message for visiting foreigners too. One of the trinkets at Wahga was a collectible pin with a shape approximating a triangle, with one point up. The left slope of the triangle was formed by a miniature dagger. The tip of the dagger was down and to the left, painted red for dripping blood. At the apex of the triangle was a hand gripping the hilt of the dagger. The hand was attached to a forearm extending down at an angle to form the right slope of the triangle. In block letters along the sleeve of the forearm was printed, in English block letters: "CRUSH INDIA." The same slogan was painted on most of the other souvenir items for sale.

16. HOW MUCH TO THE KHYBER PASS?

THE CONTRAST WITH the Indian cities was dramatic. Pakistan was a world away from its southern neighbour. There were no beggars, no wandering cows, no piles of garbage in the streets, and no ubiquitous odour of excrement. Many signs encouraged you to drink "Campa-cola." The occasional people calling "Hello" were simply greeting me, unlike the Indian touts angling for my tourist cash. Another obvious difference was that women were invisible in Pakistan, hidden away by Islam.

The strength of Islam's grip on women was weakest in the cities. In Lahore, Pakistan's second largest city, most women in the streets wore a full-body cloak called a *chador*. The chador has a hood to cover the head but leaves the face visible. In the small traditional towns like Rawalpindi and Peshawar, however, women were reduced to walking columns of fabric. Rural women wear the *burka*, a one-piece body cloak, hood, and veil completely covering the face. The burka has a small slot of mesh in front of the eyes to allow the hidden woman to see. Even wearing burkas, I rarely caught sight of women in small towns. They seemed to walk in public only when absolutely necessary, moving in groups of two or three. Women in burkas made it clear that they did not want to be photographed, either, despite the fact that a photo would not even reveal their eyes behind the dark mesh panels.

I surmised that this hiding away of women would lead to a very sexually repressed society. The local men I encountered loved to be photographed and never failed to introduce the topic of sex during small talk. One day while visiting the Lahore Museum, I met a Pakistani man in his early thirties. After I corrected him that I was not from Japan, but from Canada, the fellow blurted out: "Canada, North America, and London is a very sex country!" I could not tell whether he was envious, expressing Muslim disapproval, or merely stating a fact.

Back at the guest house in Lahore, I met an American girl who couldn't wait to leave Pakistan after entering from Amritsar less than a week before. She complained bitterly about how she had been leered at, cat-called, groped, pinched, and spat upon for three days straight. She was a slim blue-eyed Caucasian, with shoulder-length, light brown hair, and (at least in the hostel) she displayed her bare arms. Of course, it was ridiculously hot. But she was also travelling as a solo young woman in a deeply Islamic country where women covered up. I listened sympathetically but thought, *And you were expecting...?*

The British Raj ended in 1947. Upon its departure, the British Government partitioned the Indian subcontinent into two countries, India and Pakistan. There has been much debate about whether or where the border should have been drawn, but it was clear how much the two societies had diverged since. India was predominantly Hindu, which I described earlier as a fun religion. Although there were Hindu nationalist political parties in India, there were plenty of other vibrant competing political parties for secular, communist, and special-interest groups winning seats in the Parliament of India. Pakistan, on the other hand, had a history of alternating between control by its military and control by a government closely tied to one particular religion: Islam.

At the time I was in Pakistan, its Prime Minister Nawaz Sharif was promoting a bill to enforce religious Shariah law. Sharif wanted to amend Pakistan's constitution so that the 1,400-year-old code of Islam would be the supreme law of the land. In 1991, the Pakistani people were flirting with government by religion, while I had grown up in a Canada where everyone accepted that religious beliefs had little to do with law-making.

Under Shariah law, thieves have their hands cut off, someone having sex outside of marriage gets a public whipping or stoning, and anyone criticizing Islam is to be executed. Women must hide their faces and stay indoors. A man can get rid of his wife by reciting "I divorce thee" three times. Why would any modern population embrace these harsh punishments and gender inequality? The explanation I received was that it would only be through strict adherence to Shariah that Pakistan could hope to combat endemic corruption, abuse of authority by government officials, and blatantly unchecked criminals who had money, power, and guns. I have since, over the years, met immigrants in Canada from Islamic Middle East countries. Many of these immigrants shared similar stories with me about how their homeland villages had been over-run by lawless scoundrels, but when the Muslim zealots arrived to take over and started chopping off hands for stealing, local residents welcomed the resulting order and security.

Pakistan definitely felt more dangerous for travelers than India. The Pakistan tourist board warned visitors to avoid the lost city of Mohenjo Daro. That is a major archeological site I had wanted to visit in the country's central corridor. Mohenjo Daro is an ancient mud-brick city from the mysterious Indus Valley civilization of 2,500 BCE. The city streets are in a grid with a drainage system. Almost every house had a built-in bathroom. But there were no temples, nor any palace. No one knows who lived in Mohenjo Daro, or why the Indus Valley civilization collapsed. Every human being in that entire civilization had lived, died, and then vanished without leaving behind a clue about its heroes, adventures, or way of life.

Mohenjo Daro was abandoned, buried, and then completely forgotten until archeologists discovered it in 1921. The ruins became a major tourist attraction. Unfortunately, revenues from tourism plummeted when Pakistani bandits discovered they could kidnap foreign tourists at Mohenjo Daro for ransom money. The bandits were making this a weekly habit in the 1990s. As a result, Mohenjo Daro would remain a mystery to me, too. I decided instead to make my way northwest to visit the fabled Khyber Pass.

The Khyber Pass is part of the historic Silk Road trading route between two great civilizations: China and Rome. Silk, ceramics, and spices went west from Beijing in mighty China; wool, wine, and gold went east from Constantinople of the Roman Empire. Made famous today by the writing of Marco Polo, the Silk Road was traveled by merchant caravans of trade goods for centuries. The route also allowed for the exchange of religions, technologies, and diseases. The Khyber Pass through the Hindu Kush Mountains is where Silk Road travelers crossed between modern Pakistan in the southeast and Afghanistan in the northwest.

The Khyber Pass lies just inside the border of Afghanistan. Control of the pass meant control of trade and transportation. For centuries, local Afghanistan warlords claimed ownership of the Khyber Pass, charging Silk Road travelers a toll to travel safely through the mountains as a main source of income.

Afghanistan's recent history before my visit was turbulent. In 1979, Afghanistan's newly elected communist government collapsed, confronted by capitalists who were resisting communist changes, and extreme Islamic religious leaders seeking Islamic changes. Communist Russia, on the northern border of Afghanistan, feared the rise of both capitalism and Muslim extremists in its neighbour. Russia decided to invade. Russia's war in Afghanistan lasted ten years. By 1991, the Russians had finally pulled out. Then, with their common enemy gone, rival Afghanistan groups started fighting each other. Afghanistan was in the throes of civil war, and I would not be visiting. But I would come close.

Peshawar is the frontier town on the Pakistan side closest to the Khyber Pass. In the 1600s, Afghanistan kings had invaded, captured Peshawar, and used it as their winter palace for two hundred years. Afghanistan lost Peshawar back to Pakistan when the British East India Company arrived, and the British Raj covered the entire Indian sub-continent.

From Lahore, I made my way by minivan through Rawalpindi to Peshawar. Small towns like Rawalpindi and Peshawar are a world away from cosmopolitan Lahore. Most of the men are Pashtun. I saw many of them casually walking the streets carrying rifles. It seemed that the men spent much of their days in ubiquitous tea shops, chatting and enjoying tea, *dhal, chappatis,* and rice. The women, on the other hand, were only fleetingly glimpsed as they scurried about in small groups covered in full burka. For photographic proof that women even existed in this part of the world, I resorted to taking pictures covertly from a window on the second floor of a tea shop.

Even on the Pakistan side, the Khyber Pass was a no-go zone for do-it-yourself backpacker tourists. Neither the British nor the Pakistan government has ever fully tamed Peshawar in the rebellious North-West Frontier Province. The area has been ruled by the local Pashtun tribal chiefs since time immemorial. The Pakistan government decided it was too dangerous for foreign tourists to visit the Khyber Pass without an armed police escort. However, I knew that the local buses stopping in Peshawar carried civilians to, and probably across, the pass and the international border into Afghanistan for work and business. And that bus trip would cost pennies compared to the cost of arranging an armed escort.

I succumbed to temptation.

It was an easy matter to wander down the next morning to the Peshawar bus park and ask for a bus headed to the pass. I was dressed in light-weight cotton cargo pants, a t-shirt, and sneakers. All I carried for day excursions during this part of my journey was a small black nylon pouch on a shoulder strap. The pouch was barely large enough to hold my SLR camera, a couple of extra canisters of film, and my passport. After talking with one or two of the drivers at the bus park, I was directed to a half-full vehicle. The response from its jovial round-faced driver standing outside was a grin and vigorous nodding.

"Khyber Pass? You want to see Khyber Pass? Come!" the bus driver said in English, beaming. He looked over his shoulder and called out something in Urdu (or Pashto, the local language of the North-West Frontier Province). A few bystanders laughed, but not in a mean-spirited way.

The driver took my proffered ten Pakistani rupees, about forty cents in Canadian currency. He gestured for me to board the bus. I have no idea whether I paid any more than the other passengers. It was impossible to know, since the bus route went through several villages. Each person would pay a different fare depending on how far that individual was travelling that day.

The bus was a dilapidated affair with the standard too-small seats and window glass opaque with road grime. Most of the windows were rolled down for natural air-conditioning. I got plenty of looks as I boarded. All the other riders were men as well, dressed in the same plain white or beige long tunic and matching billowing pants. These men had black hair and beards and deep-set dark eyes glinting with amusement. When I took a seat, the man seated behind me tapped me on the shoulder. He asked, "Japan?" They did not see many non-Caucasian tourists in this part of the world.

The bus set off, proceeding along a ribbon of highway through a landscape of rocks, stones, and dust. After every twenty or thirty minutes, we would pass a military checkpoint. Just before the first checkpoint, the Pakistanis seated around me gently pushed on the back of my head, forcing me to duck as the bus slowed. They shushed me, and made gestures urging me to feign sleep.

An armed officer came aboard and paced the length of the aisle inspecting passengers. Apparently satisfied, he exchanged a few words in Urdu with the driver, and stepped off the vehicle. We continued along the road.

Nearing the second checkpoint, the passenger behind me reached forward over the top of my seat and rolled up my window. He was using the dusty glass to obscure me from prying eyes outside. The man seated on my left motioned for me to duck my head, saying something in Urdu. This time, a length of fabric appeared, donated by some unknown passenger, and several hands reached out to deftly wrap my head in a turban. The disguise was administered with gentle conspiratorial laughter. When we stopped, another military man with a rifle slung over his shoulder came on the bus. He scanned the passengers on both sides as he, too, walked the length of the aisle. With my turbaned head lowered, I apparently escaped his attention as well.

After these inspections, I was beginning to think that taking a local bus to the Khyber Pass was not such a good idea. But we continued down the road for another half hour, while I watched the parched and unchanging landscape that resembled nothing less than an endless stone farm. The skies were grey but there was zero chance of rain. I noticed small white sentry boxes on some of the hilltops. They appeared empty now but were originally built and used by the Pakistan army.

At the third checkpoint, the soldier did not come on board. Instead, he walked around the exterior of the bus, looking in carefully through each window. My window was closed again, but this time the machine gun-toting soldier paused directly outside of where I was sitting. My head was down, and I was dutifully studying the floor. I heard the footsteps outside come to a stop. Then the soldier's finger tapped on the glass. I looked up to see the man staring at me intently but without malice. He jerked his thumb to indicate that I should get off the bus.

Ironically, I was hassled getting on the bus in Thailand and Nepal because I was mistaken for a local resident but kicked off the bus in Pakistan because I could not pass for a local resident.

I don't recall that soldier saying a word. He probably saw it as pointless, since I didn't look like I could speak Urdu. I simply stood in the road as my happy-go-lucky bus driver pulled away. In a short time, another bus from the opposite direction pulled in and came to a stop. The soldier put a hand on my shoulder and firmly guided me onto the arriving bus. I didn't even need to show a ticket or pay. The new driver simply glanced at the soldier waving his rifle and then motioned me on board to find an empty seat. I headed back in the direction from which I had come.

Thus ended my cheap trip to the Khyber Pass.

Back at the hostel in Peshawar, I met up that evening with Gareth, a philosophical fellow from New Zealand. Gareth wore billowing rayon pants with a sky-blue tropical beach pattern and a rope drawstring around the waist. He had flip flops on his feet. Looking erudite in round spectacles with thin black wire frames, he intoned, "True wisdom only comes from years of travel." We agreed to split the cost for an escorted jeep ride to see the Khyber Pass. The next day, we went to the local police station to try to arrange another, officially sanctioned, trip. The officers inspected our passports, took a fee in US dollars, and told us to report back in the morning.

The jeep ride with the armed guards on the Torkham Highway was much faster than the bus trip I had taken two days before. Even this short segment of the Silk Road from Peshawar to the pass was steeped in history. We headed northwest, past the village of Jamrud. Fifteen kilometres later, we came to the narrowest point of the route, Ali Masjid. This location was in a canyon, famous because originally it was so narrow that two fully-loaded camels could not walk past each other. Forts were built at this strategic site, first by the Afghans when they still controlled Peshawar, and then by the British. Continuing along the highway, we passed rows of "dragon's teeth." These were boulder-sized concrete pyramids installed by British soldiers to block the passage of German tanks. During World War II, Britain was afraid Germany would invade India from the north-west through the Khyber Pass. In the jeep, we proceeded on through Landi Kotal at 1,200 meters above sea level. Landi Kotal, the highest point between Peshawar and the pass itself, is a town historically famous for smugglers of hashish and weapons.

Our last stop without an Afghanistan visa was the Michni checkpoint, high on a hill manned by Pakistani soldiers. We had travelled fifty-eight kilometres west from Peshawar. From the checkpoint, we looked down into the wide and barren valley of the Khyber Pass. It was easy to imagine Genghis Khan and his Mongol hordes galloping through on horseback, numberless in number. Or I could visualize slow merchant caravans of camels piled high with trade goods, trekking in both directions on the endless road snaking along the north side of the valley. At the bottom, we could see the town of Torkham, situated on the actual border between the two countries. Torkham looked deceptively peaceful.

Thirty years later, the Khyber Pass is the scene of active conflict between local Pashtun warlords, Taliban extremists, the Pakistan army, and US drone strikes. No one is visiting as a tourist these days.

The author at the Michni Checkpoint, Pakistan, overlooking the Khyber Pass.

17. GIRLFRIENDS IN THE WEST

AFTER MY TRIP to the Khyber Pass, I decided to travel to Darra, a dusty, ramshackle one-street town forty kilometres south of Peshawar. The town's attraction was the curious business of hand-crafting and selling small arms. Darra is part of a regional cottage industry making counterfeit weapons. Using local scrap metal, such as old car parts and railway spikes, village blacksmiths fashion what are known to gun collectors as "Khyber Pass Copies."

The bright warm afternoon was punctuated by the sounds of hammering, filing, and sawing of metal gun components. Walking along the street, I saw rows of what looked like open garage spaces. Each was a combination retail store and weapons manufacturing facility. Products on display for sale included hand-made Lee-Enfield rifles, Beretta hand guns, and AK-47 machine guns. They were all copied in minute detail from originals that had come from first the British army, then from other foreign armies or mercenaries. The Darra gunsmiths even copy the markings on the original weapons. I saw spelling mistakes or flipped English letters on some of the guns. In every shop, men were sitting or squatting, working with hand tools on gun parts held in metal vices.

At first, I couldn't believe these people were actually making machine guns by hand. But then again, I realized that's how guns must have been made in the past, since early muskets and pistols were first developed in Europe. Occasionally, a Darra gunsmith would step out into the street and fire a gun into the air, apparently testing his handiwork. I didn't see anyone buying. There were there no signs posted about permits or regulations to carry or export these weapons out of Pakistan. Or maybe the signs were there, written in Urdu, and I just couldn't read them.

Gunsmiths in Darra, Pakistan.

I hung around town watching the gun-making process and bought a few samosas to snack on while I explored. I was approached by a local resident who quietly offered to sell me hashish, which I declined. At one of the gun shops, a boy just starting to grow fuzz on his upper lip handed me various firearms to inspect. He seemed especially proud of a "pen gun," which, of course, looked like a stainless-steel ball-point pen. I took the time to handle and admire the workmanship but had no intention of purchasing the souvenir. Then the young salesman asked, "Want to fire AK-47?"

What the heck, 200 Pakistani rupees (less than eight dollars Canadian) to shoot a machine gun? We left the shop and took the AK-47 a few blocks away. Rounding a corner, I found myself facing a desolate rocky hillside directly behind a row of buildings. My guide walked thirty feet ahead and carefully balanced three empty soft-drink bottles on top of a large boulder at shoulder height. He had obviously used this spot before. Returning to my side, he then showed me how to release the safety catch on the rifle and stepped behind me out of the line of fire.

I had never fired a gun in my life. I had only read about recoil. I had seen movies with shooters wearing ear protection at the shooting range, and where first-time shooters "can't hit a barn door." I lifted the AK-47 to sight along its barrel at one of the bottles. I held my breath and gently squeezed the trigger. The weapon was fully automatic, meaning that it fired continuously until I released the trigger. I missed the bottle I had aimed for. But the shots were not as loud as I'd anticipated, and the recoil not as jolting.

Emboldened, I raised the machine gun again. This time, I took more careful aim at the bottles. *Bang, bang, bang, bang, bang!* I emptied the clip in what seemed like a few seconds, and I was able to hit not a single bottle.

It was weeks later that I realized I could not remember any "ping" or dust from bullets ricocheting off the rocks surrounding the glass targets I missed. I hadn't noticed any spent bullet casings falling to the ground either. Then again, all my so-called knowledge was from what I had seen in the movies. More importantly, I also learned later that the quality of a Khyber Pass Copy ranged from a near-factory specification product to one that exploded when you pulled its trigger. At least the AK-47 hadn't blown up in my face.

There were no other backpackers with me on the bus from Darra returning to Peshawar. The only things outside the windows were passing stones and desert, without even the occasional stunted tree or scraggly bush. I was daydreaming about where I could live near the water when I returned to Canada. Unexpectedly, the bus slowed for a military check. There was no village in sight. We were stopped by a jeep with a couple of rifle-toting soldiers.

One of those soldiers came aboard and exchanged some words with the driver. None of the local Pakistani passengers showed the least bit of anxiety or interest at this interruption. The soldier calmly marched down the aisle straight to my seat and motioned for me to stand up. He pointed to my camera bag. I handed it to him without protest.

The soldier looked in every compartment, pulling out my wallet, vaccination-record booklet, and passport. He flipped through my passport and found the necessary visa stamps. He then pulled out my camera and uncoupled the lens barrel from the camera body, peering through the lens for anything hidden in the barrel. He was clearly familiar with the lens-attachment mechanism from previous practice.

Satisfied that there was nothing stashed in the bag or camera, he placed them on the seat. Then he patted me down in front and back, searching for hidden containers or objects. I had to turn my pockets inside out. Finally, he motioned for me to sit back down, and take off my sneakers.

The soldier ran a finger down the sole of each of my socked feet, tickling me through the fabric. Then he inspected and palpated the insides of my shoes. He didn't flinch at the foot odour. He didn't have any hand-sanitizing lotion to use afterwards, either.

No drugs. He nodded politely, and then left the bus.

As the engine restarted and we pulled away, I thought about that evening passing the joint at the Planters' Club only a few weeks earlier in Darjeeling, India. I had no idea how strict the laws were in Pakistan against marijuana. I can't recall who supplied the marijuana in Darjeeling, but I was happy I didn't carry my own personal supply.

Once back in Peshawar, I met up with Gareth again for dinner. The next day, we set off to explore the old town, with its tea shops and an intriguing lane of gold shops. We had no understanding of gold jewelry quality. We had no way to verify the actual gold content in the thousands of rings, chains, and pendants on display, and no intention of purchasing gold. Nevertheless, every Peshawar merchant eagerly invited us into his shop. Eventually, Gareth and I did find ourselves inside a gold shop. We sat across a table from one Fazal-e-Karim.

Fazal was talkative and solicitous, and appeared to be in his late twenties. His father owned the shop, which also sold antiques. Fazal was convinced that any worn-looking Pakistani artifact of unknown origin could be sold for thousands of dollars "in the West." He treated us to endless cups of apple juice, *naan*, *dhal*, and tea. Fazal explained that, having learned English, he was anxious to line up a sponsorship "in the West" to earn a Master's degree in English studies. He confided that he felt fettered by Pakistani culture. He was eager to pass whatever exams were necessary to obtain a sponsorship. Gareth and I were unable to puzzle out the nature of this sponsorship Fazal had in mind, or who would be providing it "in the West."

Fazal was matter-of-fact and open, too, about how all men have sexual needs. Without any prodding, he related how he had just returned from Lahore, after relieving himself of some money and semen. No, he would never engage in such activities with his girlfriend. Never! Had we ever touched our girlfriends "in the West?"

Gareth and I had quite the conversation with Fazal over more than an hour. However, we backpackers merely touched the tea to our lips without actually drinking. We did nibble on the food. We felt secure in the belief, probably wrong, that it would be difficult to drug and overcome both of us at once. We had heard tales of trusting backpackers waking up after these visits of hospitality, separated from their money and belongings.

We left Fazal's shop without buying anything. We made no promises about sponsorships. Once outside, Gareth and I regretted that perhaps we had behaved poorly. Were we justified in suspecting that Fazal and every local Pakistani was trying to rip us off? We chatted about the challenge for backpackers to be constantly alert during extended travel, taking precautions against petty crime, and yet remaining open to meeting and getting to know the local people of the places we were visiting. After all, interacting with the locals was one of the main objectives of travelling in the first place.

At length, we returned to the hostel. As we were passing one of the guestrooms, we heard a low moaning. Concerned, we knocked on the door. Silence. Then the rustling of someone moving about inside.

"Are you okay in there?" I called.

More low moaning and jumbled speech. We could only understand the last word: "out."

But there was a padlock on the outside of the door, locking the occupant inside. We learned that the padlock belonged to the man inside, and he no longer had the key. Gareth left to fetch the hostel manager. I stayed and reassured the prisoner that help was on the way.

In short order, Gareth and the manager were back standing at the door with me. At first, the manager refused to break the lock. The hostel manager did not want to pay for a new replacement lock. Gareth and I promised that we would cover the cost, and the manager then left to fetch someone with a hammer and chisel. After this other fellow arrived with his tools, he too was reluctant to set the poor backpacker free. The man with the tools feared that he would have to pay for any damage that might be inflicted on the door while removing the lock.

Eventually Gareth and I prevailed, and the prisoner was set free. The victim was a French national, which was part of the reason for our difficulty in understanding him. His name was Gilles, and he had befriended a local fellow named Khalid. Khalid had given Gilles a guided tour of the old town. As the tour ended, Khalid had persuaded the Frenchman to buy some fresh juice from one of the market stalls: special mango juice.

The two had returned to Gilles' room at the hostel to enjoy the mango juice treat at their leisure. Unfortunately, Khalid had surreptitiously drugged the juice. Gilles was rendered unconscious for two nights and a day. Khalid robbed Gilles of cash, traveler's cheques, camera, and anything else that could be sold, and then fled after locking the sedated backpacker into the room with Gilles' own lock.

The rest of the hostel backpackers took up a collection. We provided Gilles with enough money for a couple of days while he sought help from the French consulate.

18. TRAIN ORPHAN

FROM PESHAWAR, I went back through Lahore on my way to Karachi, the largest city of Pakistan situated on the coast of the Arabian Sea. I travelled from Lahore southwest to Karachi by train.

What I remember most about the train trip is the toasting wind blowing in from the desert. There was no glass to close the windows. The passengers would have died overheating if the windows had been closed. To travel the length of Pakistan's Indus Valley Desert, I paid 155 rupees (six dollars Canadian) for train passage in second-class, sleeping on a vinyl-covered bench attached to the wall. I suffered like the other passengers in thirty-degree heat. I had unwisely decided to not wait two days until a first-class air-conditioned berth would have been available. The wind felt like hot air from a hair blow-dryer. It was only May but travelling under the sun in what was essentially a metal tube baked the sweat out of you. Just as in India before, I got filthier and filthier with dust coating every inch of exposed skin. I had learned nothing from my previous forty-three-hour train ride from Madurai to Kolkata.

Life on the Pakistan train included entertainment by cranky babies, cute-as-can-be kids, inquisitive old men, and quiet veiled women, young and old. Young men enthusiastically embraced each other while gushing about their action-movie idols, Jackie Chan, Sylvester Stallone, Chuck Norris, and Arnold Schwarzenegger.

There were no Hollywood dramas, romantic comedies, or horror movies playing in Pakistan; these genres of film did not translate well for the Muslim audience.

Several of the male occupants in my train compartment chewed *paan*, a very common habit throughout Pakistan and India. A wad of paan is made by wrapping betel leaves around an areca nut. The leafy betel vine is in the same plant family as the yaqona plant used to make the kava drink I had enjoyed on Fiji. The areca nut comes from the fruit of the areca palm tree. Both betel leaves and areca nuts are mildly addictive stimulants, like coffee.

The practice of chewing paan dates back thousands of years across Southeast Asia. Paan is widely available in ready-to-chew packets in grocery stores. There are entire plantations devoted to producing the components. After chewing, the user spits out the paan and smiles with red-stained teeth. There was a lot of paan spitting on that Pakistan train. Probably because I saw so much spitting of paan-saliva mash, I had absolutely zero desire to try it.

The journey took thirty hours, and unlike the trains in India, no food or drink was sold on board. Passengers were grateful whenever the train stopped at towns along the route where food and refreshments could be purchased from vendors inside the stations. At each stop, everyone rushed off for a drink of cooling water at public fountains installed on the platform, splashing copious amounts over faces and arms. At the first of these stops, I washed my face with relief. However, when I cupped my hands under the stream of running water to have a drink, an earnest Pakistani youth appeared at my elbow and stopped me. He shook his head and indicated through miming motions that I would get sick. Instead, he took me by the shoulder and steered me towards a refreshment vendor. My new friend purchased snacks and two bottled drinks. He handed me some of the snacks and one of the bottles. His name was Hassan, and he refused to let me help pay for these items.

Hassan's English was limited; my Urdu non-existent. We did not exchange many words, but Hassan parked himself beside me for the rest of the train ride like a guardian angel. He accompanied me at every subsequent stop and produced soap he had brought along for washing up at the train station fountains. He bartered with the snack vendors for me, so I would not pay more than the price for locals. In the evening, Hassan handed me one of his spare shirts to use as a pillow. In return, he wanted ... nothing. He did not even ask for my address. Many other locals had asked for my home address in the hope that I might be a useful contact in Canada someday in the future. Hassan's behavior was a disarming random act of kindness.

When we finally arrived at Karachi station, Hassan's eyes actually watered up. We hugged and parted. Then he simply turned and walked away. He disappeared into the station crowds.

I suspect Hassan was a Pashtun from the Northwest Frontier Province I had just been visiting. The Pashtun live by a moral code known as the *Pashtunwali*. This code of behavior requires the Pashtun to seek vengeance if any member of your family is insulted, leading to bitter family feuds that can last a century. On the other hand, the code also obligates the Pashtun to provide hospitality to all visitors without expectation of reward. I had just been the recipient of a Pashtunwali experience. Lucky for me it wasn't one of the life-threatening variety.

Before I left Karachi, I wanted to mail home a package of souvenirs, exposed canisters of camera film, and other things I didn't want to lug around anymore. Being in a modern city, the sixth largest in the world by population, I expected to visit a Karachi post office to purchase a box for mailing. I was disappointed. Pakistan postal outlets did not provide or sell cardboard boxes. Moreover, I was told to put all the items to be shipped in a *cloth bag* instead.

"Where can I get a bag?" I asked.

"Anywhere. Everywhere," said the post office clerk. "Just buy the white cotton cloth and have someone sew it up. Any of the tailors in the small shops will do it for you. They should not charge you too much money. There are probably a dozen shops around the corner where you can get it done," he said. The clerk motioned for me to step aside so he could serve the next person in line.

After leaving the post office, I spent the next two hours trudging from shop to shop, making my request to have a bag sewn, and being turned away. In fact, I was not able to locate any shopkeeper willing to sell me a bag until the middle of the afternoon the next day. I could see nothing about this particular shop that was any different from the previous dozen I'd visited, but the man inside smiled and agreed to help me immediately. The tailor sold me the white fabric and skillfully sewed it into a bag in minutes. He left one end open for the contents to be inspected by customs agents. The tailor assured me that the main Karachi post office would supply me with needle and thread to finish the job. Dubious, I thanked him, paid and left to fill my bag with the items I wanted to ship back to Canada.

Karachi's main post office was within walking distance from my hotel. I arrived clutching my bag an hour before the post office closed. Sure enough, officials inspected the items, filled out forms, and then pointed me to a table where several other people were busy sewing up their own fabric packages. My sewing job was not pretty, but it was secure. Nothing would fall out. However, I wondered how many items would survive delivery without the protection afforded by a rigid container. It cost me six Canadian dollars to send the three-pound parcel from Karachi to Toronto. Miraculously, everything inside survived intact. I have kept that cotton cloth bag to this day as a souvenir.

On June 8, 1991, my backpack was somewhat lighter when I got to the Karachi airport than when I had left Canada five months earlier. In addition to the items I'd just put in the mail, I no longer had an underwater camera (broken), or a tent and stove (given away), or half of my travel guidebooks (pitched). I replaced my heavy hardcover journal with a thin, light, soft-cover notebook. I was determined to shed every possible ounce.

The flight on Pakistan International Airlines from Karachi to Nairobi, Kenya, was full. I was seated beside an Indian businessman by the name of Arjun. He was friendly, open, and talkative. We proceeded to have a long discussion about the best way to do business. We assumed there were two prevailing business models: one of transparency, disclosure, regulations, and fair access by competitors, generally promoted by western governments; and an alternative model where transactions depended on bribery, favoritism, and corruption, endemic to developing countries. Arjun was a world traveler with business interests in Europe, the United States, East Africa, and his home country of India. I naturally expected that Arjun would prefer the western model of business.

My new Indian friend candidly informed me, however, that he preferred to do business fueled by *baksheesh*, fragrant grease, kickbacks, and bribery. In Arjun's experience, a strategic bribe to the right person allowed him to get more done, faster, and at greater personal profit than his operations in the regulated western business environment. Arjun believed that the western "level playing field" approach was merely a recipe for mediocrity. It forced him to give equal consideration to even barely competent candidates, instead of allowing him to immediately favor those whom he personally judged to be the best. Western regulations were an irritant. They fettered his ability to "jump the queue" if he wanted. And why shouldn't he be allowed to make use of his skills and connections, or spend his own hard-earned cash to outmaneuver his competitors?

Many times, my father had sadly shaken his head at my naïve belief that sensible human beings would naturally prefer a world of fairness, honesty, and regulated equal treatment. My father, Chan, never led me to believe the world was fair, that good would triumph over evil, or that honesty was the best policy. Often justice does not prevail, and Chan wasn't bitter about it. Who could be bitter about the fact that rain is wet? While he did not encourage me to cheat, Chan thought it silly to expect fair treatment to be freely given if it meant less profit for someone else.

Chan had struggled for the first half of his life to escape poverty and economic dead-ends. Growing up in rural pre-communist China, Chan almost starved to death twice as a youngster. He lived with extended family on the same pitiless plot of farmland his ancestors had toiled over to feed themselves for at least twenty-five generations. No one went to school. Everyone worked in the fields. Water was drawn from a well, and there were no doctors, no books, and no electricity. There was not even fertilizer except for the human waste produced by the villagers. In good times, Chan was able to eat dried salted fish, rice, and vegetables. That same meal was served three times a day, seven days a week, but only during good times.

Any family member who found an opportunity to escape this traditional homeland, since time immemorial, was crazy to not get the hell out. But it was not easy to escape. First, Chan immigrated to Guyana, to build up savings through a decade of menial labor. Then there were years of spirit-killing setbacks, as Chan attempted to move to Canada but could not overcome racist immigration policies aimed at keeping Chinese people out. It was only after these policies were removed in the early 1960s that Chan finally gained permission to enter Canada with his wife and two young children. Yet Chan never begrudged Canada's government for those discriminatory policies. He understood why Canada had implemented those policies in the first place.

It wasn't only the Chinese who suffered discrimination. In 1914, almost four hundred Sikh and Hindu Indians on board the steamship *Komagata Maru* were denied entry to Canada at the port of Vancouver. These British citizens were forced to sail all the way back to India and imprisoned. In 1939, over nine hundred Jews fleeing from Hitler on board the *M.S. St. Louis* were also prevented from entering Canada. They were sent back to Europe, where about a quarter of the ship's passengers ended up dying in Nazi concentration camps.

My father understood that, in most of the world, people struggle to find enough food and shelter to survive and raise children. These struggles mean that hard choices over scarce resources must be made every single day. Driven by the relentless twins of poverty and greed, an individual can only stay fed, healthy, and build personal wealth by discriminating against other families, social classes, ethnic or religious groups, or even countries competing for the same commodities or opportunities that every human being needs or wants. To treat everyone equally was, at best, foregoing the opportunity to help a loved one or a friend to get ahead in a miserable world; and at worst, stupidly putting oneself at a disadvantage, to the glee of competitors who would never return the favor.

Today, although race is not a factor, it is still difficult to immigrate to Canada. Unless you are a refugee, you must have education and skills for which the existing population cannot meet demand; or be a wealthy financial entrepreneur who can create more jobs. Fifty years ago, it was no surprise to Chan that the dominant society in Canada had felt its high standard of living threatened by the influx of too many poor and needy immigrants. Once inside the country, these desperate immigrants would take a share of the jobs and resources that are the foundations of Canada's wealth.

On that airplane from Pakistan, I was on my way to a continent afflicted by periodic famines, inter-tribal violence, and corruption for as long as anyone could remember. I wondered how fairly the people in Africa would treat me, or each other.

19. AFRICAN GAME

THE PLANE LANDED at Nairobi airport in the dead of night. After warnings from fellow travelers, discovering my pack had been broken into and ransacked by airport security, and seeing guards armed with rifles posted throughout the airport, I was preparing to stay alert in this country. All the other passengers on my flight proceeded through immigration, then customs, and then quickly disappeared. Presumably they either left with family driving them home or had enough money to call a cab to the city. On the wall next to the car rental counter, there was an electronic board listing pricey Nairobi hotels. This display had a photograph of each establishment, with a red button beside it. Pushing a button would autodial for a shuttle to come from the hotel and fetch you from the airport, for a price. Backpackers like me could afford no such luxury.

It appeared that I was the only backpacker in the airport that night, and I saw no one with whom I could split the cost of a cab. I planned instead to take an affordable bus into town at daybreak. I settled into a waiting lounge seat, where (with luck) I wouldn't get hassled by airport security. I didn't get much sleep or have much to do for the hours until dawn.

The next morning brought Sunday. I then discovered that there was no public transit serving Nairobi International Airport on Sundays anyway.

At about six a.m., I paid 300 Kenyan shillings (about fourteen Canadian dollars) for a taxi ride into town. The countryside was magical in the pinkish dawn. In contrast to Karachi, where I thought I would melt, the temperature in Nairobi was a pleasant twenty-four degrees. On a well-maintained highway, we drove past healthy-looking agricultural fields, confirming conventional wisdom that Kenya is blessed with perfect weather and fertile soil.

A couple of times, I saw giraffes marching wild through the farmlands. The animals were strikingly majestic. You could tell they were ridiculously tall from their rhythmic, almost slow-motion, swinging gait. There was a noticeable time lag from when a giraffe's hip moved at the beginning of its stride, to when the corresponding hoof so very far away at the other end of the leg finished its forward swing and finally touched the ground.

Kenya in 1991 was a model East African democracy. It would be years before the country would be rocked by the 2007 crisis of government corruption, vote rigging, and targeted killings of the ethnic Kikuyu minority. At the time of my visit, Kenya had been stable for a decade and had built a reputation of being tourist-friendly. However, I didn't find Nairobi very interesting. After checking out a few eateries, I looked for a *matutu* headed for Arusha in neighbouring Tanzania.

A matutu is a minivan used for collective transit. The matutu driver departs for a specified destination when he has picked up enough fare-paying passengers to make a profit after deducting costs for fuel, maintenance, licensing, and bribes. I never saw a single female matutu driver. Gender equality was not a social priority in East Africa. And you never knew what time a matutu would depart. I've even wondered if a matutu driver would cancel a trip, giving refunds, if not enough passengers turned up. That never happened to me, although on several occasions I waited almost two hours in a matutu park for enough passengers to show.

I found the Nairobi intercity bus park and settled into a matutu headed for Namanga, a town on the Kenyan border with Tanzania. Doors on both sides to the minivan were open. A well-dressed man in a dark brown suit was already sitting on the bench behind the driver's seat. His nose was buried in a newspaper. I was the second paying occupant and took a spot on the bench opposite to the businessman. Two more passengers clambered into the bench seat at the rear. After a few minutes, a man introducing himself as the manager of the bus company seated himself on my right. The manager asked me to slide towards the centre.

The manager shook my hand with a broad grin. "Are you going to Arusha, to climb the mountain?" he asked.

"Yes," I replied. "That's the plan. I'm hoping to get up Mount Kilimanjaro and to visit the Serengeti game park while I'm in Tanzania."

"*Hakuna matata* (no problem)," he said. "There are many companies in Arusha where you can get a guide to take you up the mountain, and it's easy to book a safari trip. Have you changed money? You need to have 5,000 Tanzanian shillings to enter Tanzania. Not Kenyan shillings. No one takes Kenyan money in Tanzania. I can give you a good rate to change."

"Ah, no, I think I'll be okay," I demurred. I had exchanged enough currency at the bank in Nairobi to cover the matutu ride and costs for the first few days in Tanzania.

"You should change all your money now. I can give you a good rate, five to one," he persisted. "There are no places to change money at the border."

The businessman on my left looked up from his paper. "You change at five to one?" he asked. "That's a very good rate. Can you change 1,000 Kenyan shillings for me?" he asked, pulling out a wad of currency from his pocket and waving it.

"Me, too! I want to change money too," said one of the passengers behind me.

"And me," said the last passenger. "I didn't know you need 5,000 Tanzanian shillings to get across," he added.

All three of the other passengers began counting out Kenyan bank notes for the manager to exchange. The manager pulled out a hefty wad of Tanzanian bills and began counting as well. Hands reached across me and over the seats to complete the transactions. I didn't need any more Tanzanian currency and looked away, pulling out the paperback novel I was reading at the time. I also carried a number of bills in US currency. I knew the American bills would be easy to exchange if I needed emergency cash later from less conventional money changers. Around me in the matutu, there were muttered thanks as the currency transactions were completed.

Outside, some of the matutus started their engines and departed noisily. New matutus arrived to replace those that left. I wondered if they were headed to different towns, or if I had just picked a dud matutu to Namanga that all the locals knew to avoid. Time passed without anything more unpleasant than boredom. There were no mosquitoes or obnoxious smells. The temperature remained a pleasant twenty-three degrees in overcast skies. I continued reading my book.

Twenty minutes later, I looked up and realized that I was now alone in the minivan. The manager and currency-exchanging passengers had all quietly melted away while I had been absorbed in my book. Over the next hour, genuine passengers started trickling into the matutu. The driver appeared from somewhere when all the passenger spots were full. Without much ceremony and less conversation, the driver collected our fares. He started up the engine, and we left the parking lot.

At Namanga two hours later, I entered the queue and presented my passport. The border official did not hassle me. My passport was stamped and returned, and I walked through the building into Tanzania. There was no requirement to be in possession of

5,000 Tanzanian shillings. I saw there was a money exchange wicket inside the Tanzania border building. The posted rate for Kenyan shillings was more than five to one, better than what the matutu "manager" had offered. I went to find a connecting matutu to Arusha.

Arriving in Arusha that afternoon, I did the by-now-familiar walkabout in search of a place to stay. Small towns are easy for backpackers to get oriented and inspect several prospective hostels on foot, but sometimes the choice of accommodation is limited. As well as comfort and budget, security is always top-of-mind in evaluating rooms. You want to feel safe from a break-in while asleep, and confident that your belongings, including irreplaceable souvenirs you've collected, can be left in the room while you are away during the day.

I chose a small hotel and settled in. Next, I found a restaurant for a late lunch of curry chicken, rice with peas and carrots, and beer. After lunch, I proceeded to look for some means to visit Serengeti National Park.

The sign by the front door read: "Taurus Tour Company." Posted in the window was a list of tour packages on offer, including both multi-day safaris to the game parks and guided treks up Mount Kilimanjaro. Inside, behind a large desk, bare except for a few brochures in one corner, sat Clemence. He was dressed in a tan-colored suit, white shirt, and tie. Like every other African man I had seen, his hair was in tight, short natural curls close to his skull. Clemence was a soft-spoken man of medium build. He was speaking in English with a slight accent to two other tourists, apparently just finishing up with them. The British couple in their mid-thirties stood up, shook hands with Clemence, and smiled as they squeezed past me and out the door.

I told Clemence of my two objectives. We discussed dates, logistics, and what would be included in the price. I agreed to pay a bit more, because I would be alone in a tent on the safari, instead of sharing for double-occupancy. In addition to visiting the Serengeti, my four-day safari would include visits to Lake Manyara National Park and the Ngorongoro Crater Conservation Area. Clemence arranged for connecting transportation for me after the safari, from the game parks to Moshi. There, I would find a different tour group assembling for a trek up Mount Kilimanjaro. I paid Clemence in US dollars and then left to enjoy Arusha. I would return with my gear in a couple of days to meet my safari group and head off for adventure in a Land Rover.

20. UNDER THE ACACIA TREE

THE VIEW FROM the entry gates to Serengeti National Park was not disappointing. We clambered out of the Land Rovers to stretch our legs and looked down from Naabi Hill to the vast golden grassland, sparsely dotted with photogenic yellow-barked Acacia trees displaying their distinctive flat tops. Our party consisted of two Land Rovers with eight western tourists, and three Tanzanians: Wilfred our guide, a driver for the second vehicle, and a cook.

The vehicle of choice for safaris in East Africa appeared to be the Land Rover, an exceedingly tough sport utility vehicle built by the British Land Rover Company. Although today the company has transformed its products into high-end luxury vehicles, the original Land Rover was designed for a niche market: to survive rough off-road use by farmers. The design turned out to be perfectly suited for the abuse of the African wilderness. The only adaptation needed to use the vehicle on safaris was a metal cage welded onto the roof. Our packs, gear, and camping meals were trussed securely with cords within the cage.

The park gates were still closed. They would not open until six a.m., and we had arrived a few minutes early to maximize our game-viewing time. The vehicles came to a stop and pulled up to the side of the road next to the gates. Wilfred stepped out to talk to the park rangers stationed at the gatehouse. Unfortunately, when Wilfred returned, he had to inform us that the Taurus Tour

Company was banned from entering the Serengeti for delinquency of fee payment. The park rangers would not let us in.

A collective grumble arose from the tourists. Wilfred told us not to worry. Then he drove off alone in one of the vehicles back towards a town with a telephone to resolve the matter. I settled onto the ground with an acacia tree at my back, unperturbed on this beautiful pleasant morning. When one of my safari companions remarked on how well I was taking the setback, I explained that I was happy I wasn't stuck at a train station in the middle of the night, fending off beggars and self-important Indian security officials. I had gotten used to unexpected half-day waits over months of third-world travel.

Today, the term "third world" is frequently used to describe the under-developed countries of the world, especially those with widespread poverty. The phrase was originally coined after World War II during the Cold War years that followed. Third-world nations were distinct from both the "first world" capitalist western and European countries, and the "second world" communist group of Russia, China, Cuba, and Eastern bloc countries. The military forces of third-world countries were aligned with neither NATO and capitalism, nor the Soviet Union and communism. It just so happened that most of those military neutrals were impoverished nations.

Over an hour later, we finally heard the rumble of Wilfred's Land Rover returning. The guards unlocked and pulled back the gates, and we were on our way. Wilfred did not divulge the details of what arrangements or bribes had been required.

On that multi-day safari, we visited not only the Serengeti but also Lake Manyara National Park and the Ngorongoro Crater. Lake Manyara was covered with millions of flamingoes, living placidly with enormous hippos that tiptoed through the water among the birds. The nineteen-kilometre wide Ngorongoro Crater, another UNESCO World Heritage site, was home to the highest density of lions in Africa. We were able to draw quite close to three lionesses chowing down on a bloody Cape buffalo they had recently dispatched. From our vantage point in the cars, the portion of the buffalo visible above the tall grass looked like giant barbecued ribs dripping with sauce.

We saw only one elephant. Some of the tourists in our group spoke of seeing huge herds of a hundred elephants in the national parks of other African countries. It was interesting that, by the 1990s, one hundred elephants were considered a huge herd, while only a few decades earlier, herds of 100,000 migrating elephants were common.

It had been one of my lifelong dreams to visit Serengeti Park, ever since watching wildlife documentaries about it as a youngster. I can still remember host Marlin Perkin's voice announcing "Dawn on the Serengeti Plains" in the opening scenes of Mutual of Omaha's *Wild Kingdom* television show. I'd grown up fearing that elephants, rhinos, and tigers would be extinct by the time I was an adult.

Today, thirty years after my African safari, rhinos are in fact extinct in the wild, with only a few thousand surviving protected in national parks. Wildlife biologists predict that tigers will also be extinct in the wild in less than twenty years. Humans have not been able to curb their penchants for poaching or wildlife habitat destruction in such a short span of time.

Including our days in the Serengeti, our safari group was treated to sightings of giraffes, impalas, gazelles, hyenas, dik-diks, monkeys, vultures, a leopard lazing on a tree limb high above, herds of zebras drinking at a river, and the famous migration of the wildebeest. We even encountered some of the indigenous Maasai tribespeople, who would let you to take their photographs for a fee.

I have seen the Serengeti National Park at night in a lightning storm too.

Giraffes in the Serengeti, Tanzania.

After recovering from the rainstorm by spending the night at the Serena Lodge, we resumed the safari on the following morning. By midday, the wildlife had concealed itself from the withering sun on the plains, and we returned to the Serena Lodge for lunch. After the meal, our party loitered at the hotel another two hours. We were waiting until the hottest part of the day was past and the animals would come out of hiding. I took a solitary walk around the exterior of the building, hoping for something worth capturing on film. I photographed a colorful iguana blending into pink and purple rocks on the ground. Then, behind the hotel kitchen area, I was astonished to see a lone buffalo perhaps fifty feet away, grazing in the tall grass.

I already had my camera in hand. After stopping short in surprise, I took a few slow, careful steps towards the animal to get the closest shot possible. After my third or fourth step, the buffalo stopped chewing and raised his head, becoming completely still, watching me.

I don't remember any breeze or any sound. I must have been standing there for ten minutes, focusing, playing with my polarizing filter, framing and cropping down for the best shot, and just observing this wonderfully exotic animal. This was the time before unlimited digital camera memory. I was rationing expensive cellulose triacetate film; I had a roll of twenty-four or thirty-six photographs for every two weeks and each shot was precious. Finally, I snapped a couple of photos, and turned to re-enter the hotel. I was surprised to see Wilfred standing a few paces away, lowering his rifle. He gave me a broad grin, and when I asked what kind of animal I had discovered, he answered nonchalantly, "Cape buffalo." Wilfred left to return the rifle to the front seat of the Land Rover parked on the other side of the hotel.

In addition to Wilfred, I had had a larger audience. Duncan told me how he and a number of other guests had seen me discover the buffalo, watching from the safety of the hotel dining area through a window. Wilfred had hurried to retrieve his rifle from the car. While I was fiddling with my camera polarizer and zoom lens, Wilfred was sighting a shot at the buffalo along the barrel of his gun. I did not know that the Cape buffalo is unpredictable, dangerous, and said to have killed more big game hunters than any other animal in Africa. Apparently, I'd almost been the target of a charging Cape buffalo.

Cape Buffalo at the Serena Lodge, Tanzania.

21. THE EIGHTH PORTER

THE SUMMIT OF Mount Kilimanjaro is at 5,896 meters above sea level, about half a kilometre higher than the lookout on Gokyo Ri in Nepal. Kilimanjaro has three peaks, the highest being Kibo, which can be reached without technical mountain-climbing skills. While the backpacker trekking strategy in Nepal was to ascend slowly over many days to acclimatize and avoid altitude sickness, the strategy at Kilimanjaro was to go up fast and then back down faster, before you were killed by altitude sickness.

For the trek up Kilimanjaro, I was in a group of six tourists, and we were supported by nine Tanzanians. In addition to me, the tourists included Henrik and Christina, a young couple from Denmark; Doctors Ian and Tara from New Zealand; and their friend Cameron, also a Kiwi. Henrik and Christina liked to talk politics, while Ian and Cameron entertained us with juggling acts every day. The plan was to reach the summit in three days and then descend on the following two. We were accompanied by local guide Majunga, a cook, and seven (!) porters. Majunga was the only one of the Africans who spoke much English.

On the first day after the short drive from Moshi, we met our Tanzanian support team waiting with many baskets of food at the Kilimanjaro park gate. Accompanied by Majunga, the tourists then started up on foot following the Marangu route, the easiest and most popular route to Kibo peak. We started off ahead of the porters, but within minutes the pack of porters passed us on the trail at a trot while balancing heavy baskets on their heads. We would not see any of them again until we reached the first set of huts. In addition to our supplies of food and water, the porters carried all the tourists' backpacks of personal belongings. These African men wore an assortment of worn-out sneakers or even flip-flops. Yet the porters were glad to be working; a throng of would-be porters had swarmed Majunga at the park gate, hoping to be added to our team.

We walked uphill through a lush and damp rainforest at the base of the mountain, full of chattering baboons and monkeys. The trees, mostly East Africa camphorwood, were covered in mossy beards. With tree roots, mud, rocks and ferns underfoot, the surroundings resembled a Canadian west coast rainforest more than the jungle of Tarzan. Once again, I was grateful I had my heavy but reliable leather boots.

Three hours later, we emerged to an area of low shrubs and strange plants known as tree groundsels. A groundsel looks like a thick tree trunk up to about ten feet high, topped with a ball of spikey green leaves all pointed upwards. The groundsels made the area look prehistoric, like the setting for a dinosaur movie. We were at an elevation of about 2,700 meters, and had views spanning from the Maundi crater on Kilimanjaro all the way down to the plateau below.

In the middle of the afternoon, we arrived at the Mandara huts. By 1991, the Tanzanian government had built enough solar-powered trekking huts to accommodate a staggering two hundred visitors. No doubt there are even more huts crammed at Mandara today. At the time my group was visiting, the population there numbered only twenty or so foreigners, supported by an army of Tanzanian porters. I was told that by mid-August Mandara would be full every night.

On the second day, the weather gods were generous during a leisurely six-hour hike under clear skies. The ascent was very gradual. We passed scrubby vegetation in sunshine, with brief walks through the occasional cloud rolling in to kiss the mountain. Towards dusk, we reached the Horombo huts at 3,700 meters in elevation. The sun on the horizon became blindingly bright before fading to a pale pink disk, and then the night sky filled with brilliant stars. From the huts, you could see the electric lights of Moshi far below. Up to this point, the journey had been a cake walk compared to trekking in Nepal. Especially since our packs were being carried up by porters.

The good weather continued to hold on day three. Sparse alpine vegetation gave way to a red dust desert. Ice-capped Kibo summit was within sight up ahead and drawing steadily closer, while Mawenzi peak, the second highest of the three Kilimanjaro peaks, loomed behind us. Previous visitors had arranged rocks in the desert to form words on the ground, including "Australia," "Hello Africa," and many words in foreign languages. The wind got stronger as we went higher and became numbingly cold. The only animal life we spotted was the occasional field mouse. By four p.m. we reached the Kibo Huts.

Before we had set out from Moshi, our group of six tourists had discussed concerns about food safety on the multi-day ascent. We had agreed with our guide, Majunga, that in order to minimize the risk of food poisoning, we would have chicken on the first day of the trek and have vegetarian meals thereafter. We discovered, however, that chicken was a substantial part of dinner on every night. That afternoon before our third dinner, we attempted to clarify with Majunga our collective desire to skip the chicken. Majunga appeared to have difficulty understanding but eventually acquiesced. Glum, he said "No chicken," and wandered off to find our cook. A few minutes later he returned and confirmed,

"Tonight, no chicken." Then he announced, triumphant, "We will have beef!"

In order to see the sunrise at the summit, we were to start the final ascent to Kibo at midnight that night. We relaxed in the late sun before the evening meal and enjoyed Coca-Cola purchased for 800 Tanzanian shillings a bottle, or about three Canadian dollars each. Hours later, preparing for the challenge to come, I put on every stitch of clothing I had with me. I wore my shorts as an extra layer under my trousers, two t-shirts under my long-sleeved shirt and fleece sweater, and two pairs of socks on each hand to act as mittens. I hoped that the battery in my camera would not fail too quickly in the cold, protected under a rented down-filled jacket (I had long ago ditched the blue down jacket I wore in Nepal). My head was covered by my trusty Akubra hat.

Ian had brought along a supply of chemically-activated glow sticks; he'd obviously read up before leaving New Zealand and knew what conditions to expect. He generously handed out a glow stick to each of our party, juggling them first in an impromptu display of skill. At midnight, after fortifying ourselves with a cup of tea, six intrepid fools and three Tanzanian helpers set off on a hellish journey. Our group proceeded to shuffle up the final long sand and gravel slope to Kibo in the dark. It was freezing, but fortunately the moon was nearly full and there was no wind.

Any conversation amongst us quickly fell off as we conserved energy, trudging uphill in the thin mountain air. We reached Gilman's point, barely noticing as we passed the picturesque point in darkness, pressing on through fatigue and increasing nausea caused by the altitude. Our three guides ululated to each other. Their calls were to both cheer our spirits and locate each other in the dark, keeping the tourist group together and herding us like sheepdogs. The tourists gasped for oxygen that wasn't there. Our guides were upbeat and sympathetic. *"Pole-pole* (slowly)" they advised.

Walking up loose gravel meant that for each stride up you would slide half a pace backwards and down. For every step, there was a crunch as your weight displaced the gravel, then a swish as the loose rocks rolled a little way downhill. The only sounds were the tourists' ragged breathing, the crunch and swish of everyone's steps, and the ululating of the guides. After four hours, my fatigue and nausea were joined by stomach cramps and frozen fingers. The sounds of the night were joined by a pounding in my head.

Our guides stopped us for a break and provided hot lemon tea from thermos bottles. The next two hours would be the most exhausting, fighting through lack of oxygen and dizziness. Some of our party vomited along the way, but everyone persisted. Our guides caught the stragglers and kept us together. Those up ahead were grateful to pause and catch their breath, waiting for those behind to catch up.

At 6:15 a.m. on June 24, 1991, we stumbled up to Uhuru Point, 5,894 meters above sea level on Kibo Peak of Mount Kilimanjaro. We had made it to Uhuru in time to watch the sun rising. With my teeth-chattering, I pulled out my camera to catch the pale red disk as it emerged from a layer of cloud below us. The soft pink light revealed that we were surrounded by spectacular glacier ice. I took photos of the magnificent vista, the strangely beautiful ice cliffs, and then all the tourists passed around their cameras to get photos of themselves with the guides. All six tourists in our group had made it up. With fingers numbing fast in the chill wind, we each signed the register awaiting on a pedestal installed at the peak.

With the strengthening light of day, I walked over to the crest of the slope we had just ascended. I gazed down, staring at the full extent of the steep gravel scree, which we had zigzagged up in darkness. Only then did I truly appreciate the magnitude of our achievement. I doubled over and threw up.

Sunrise at Kibo peak on Mount Kilimanjaro, Tanzania.

Today, after thirty years of global warming, the ice at the peak of Kilimanjaro is still there. Barely. The glacier has thinned, losing more than a foot of depth every year while humans debated whether global warming was real. Scientists predict that the scattered chunks of ice remaining will be completely gone in five years. *Sic transit gloria mundi.*

No one in our trekking group was so severely affected by the altitude that they needed to rush back down. As a result, it was a bunch of happy campers on a leisurely return to the base of the mountain over the next two days. As we neared the park gates, we discussed how much to pay our Tanzanian crew in tips. Although we had paid fees already, we knew that those covered trekking permits, food, park entry, our guide, transport to and from Moshi, and only a small stipend for the porters. No one was even certain how much the cook and porters were paid, but our understanding was that most of their wage would come from "tips" after the trek was done. It was important to factor in the cost of these tips when budgeting for a trip up Kilimanjaro, but the favorable currency exchange rate was helpful. Only a few Canadian dollars would go a long way in Tanzanian shillings for an African family.

When we were collectively satisfied with the amount each person in our tour group would contribute, we divvied up the tips and presented them to the Tanzanians with hugs at the park gate. Only Majunga and another driver would accompany us in the cars back to Moshi.

Each of our Tanzanian crew looked delighted with his tip as we presented the cash. First, Majunga, our lighthearted and knowledgeable guide. Next, the cook who got an extra bonus. Then we handed out money to each of our seven hard-working porters. And then we came to the *eighth* porter. As far as any of us tourists were aware, we had been escorted up the mountain by Majunga, a cook, and seven porters. But here he was, standing quietly in line and looking a bit concerned, the eighth porter, empty handed.

It was an awkward moment. We were not sure if this was a scam, but it seemed unlikely to me. For westerners unaccustomed to a population where everyone has similar African features, it was sometimes difficult to distinguish one black individual from the next. I was skeptical that a Tanzanian scammer would take the risk that none of the tourists was certain the scammer had *not* been on the trail with us. Still, some in our party were convinced it was a scam; that this additional man had simply sauntered over from the crowd at the nearby park gate to join our group of porters when we were not looking. The tourists huddled again, and grudgingly produced enough cash to tip the eighth porter.

Our Tanzanian support crew at the Horombo huts on Mt. Kilimanjaro. Majunga, our guide, is standing third from the right. The cook is crouching and holding a white ski pole. Developing this print after returning to Canada revealed that there had been, in fact, eight porters.

When I was in graduate school in Montreal, a post-doctorate student from China confided that she had a hard time distinguishing one Caucasian person from the next. I was floored. Blonde? Brunette? Blue, brown, or grey eyes? Curly or straight hair? Wei-Chen explained that, living in China, those features do not vary from person to person. Everyone in China has straight black hair and brown eyes. Instead, people in China grow up conditioned to ignore hair and eye color. Instead, they distinguish faces by discerning the distance between a person's eyes and the width of the nose. Apparently, those measurements vary far less between Caucasians than they do between Chinese individuals. I wondered if white people all looked the same to Africans too.

22. NO SHOES, NO GIN

THE COUNTRY OF Tanzania was created by the political union of continental Tanganyika with the island of Zanzibar twenty-five kilometres off the coast. While travelling between Tanganyika and Zanzibar, I encountered a curious blend of nationalism and corrupt opportunism. Even though I would be remaining within the country of Tanzania, I had to cross a "border" and pass inspection by customs agents before embarking on the *M.V. Mungano* ferry to, or from, the island.

According to travel guidebooks, no visa was required to enter or leave Zanzibar from the mainland port city of Dar es Salaam. However, every traveler lined up before a desk of uniformed agents, who authoritatively pound a visa stamp in each traveler's passport, documenting the date of entry or exit. There was no charge to receive this visa stamp, which officially was not required. However, should you choose to visit Zanzibar without getting a visa stamp, and then return to the mainland without the stamp, you would be detained and fined on the Tanganyika side for not having a properly stamped passport.

That, at least, was the advice amongst the backpackers I met at the time. I opted for prudence and waited in line for a visa stamp.

Zanzibar island was a wondrous world away from mainland Tanzania. With a spice-island culture, Zanzibar is more Arabic and Asian than African. Instead of mainland fare of steak, bread sticks, eggs, and samosas, I enjoyed evening meals from beachside stalls selling satay in peanut sauce, roasted maize, baked cassava, fried squid, and chunks of octopus. At the time of my visit, the octopus season was closed and harvest was illegal. However, anyone could still approach the "octopus guy" at his stall in the evening market. After a quick glance in either direction, he would reach under his push-cart displaying other tasty seafoods and produce a tin large enough to hold a loaf of bread. From the tin, he would retrieve one of several one-inch-thick barbecued octopus tentacles. A hunk of octopus tentacle would be hacked off with a knife, wrapped in a square of waxed paper, and surreptitiously handed to the buyer. Delicious! But the octopus guy refused to allow his picture to be taken.

The island of Zanzibar has been inhabited by humans for at least 20,000 years. As early as the first century CE, traders from India and Arabia had arrived and used Zanzibar as a stop on their ocean voyages. The Portuguese arrived in 1498 and controlled the island for almost two hundred years, until the Muslim Sultanate of Oman took over. Wealthy Arabic merchant princes grew even more prosperous on Zanzibar by trading in ivory, cloves, nutmeg, and most importantly, slaves. By the 1850s, as many as 50,000 black slaves captured from Africa's interior would pass each year through Zanzibar slave auctions. The vast majority of these slaves were the result of Africans capturing and selling their African neighbours. The Europeans were willing to pay; the Africans were quite happy to enslave each other. The lucrative business of slavery boomed until it was ended by the British in the late 1800s, when Britain replaced Oman for control of Zanzibar.

Britain never made Zanzibar a colony, and eventually relinquished control of the island in 1963. In 1964, the independent Sultanate of Zanzibar united with Tanganyika to form the modern Republic of Tanzania. Today, Zanzibar remains almost entirely Muslim, like the Arabs in Oman, while mainland Tanzania is predominantly Christian or holding indigenous beliefs. The old part of Zanzibar City, Stone Town, consists of buildings mostly from the 1800s. Stone Town displays a unique blend of Arabic, Indian, and European styles, and has been designated as another UNESCO World Heritage site. Everywhere, the locals greeted me with a smiling "Jambo!" while I explored Stone Town's maze of markets, shops, and mosques. Most of the roads were too narrow for cars and full of bicycles and motorcycles.

After a few days in Stone Town, it was time to leave for one of the island's beachside villages. I was looking forward to chartering a *dhow*, a traditional single-sailed boat, to go snorkeling in the warm turquoise waters of the Indian Ocean. The evening before leaving the city, I joined a group of backpackers organizing a party at the Africa House Hotel. Guests could watch the sunset over the ocean from a wide uncovered balcony. The hotel, which used to be the English Club, featured a gentleman's cloak room and ladies' powder room, and was reputed to serve the best gin and tonics on the island.

Africa House was a backpacker favourite, but it came with one wrinkle. There was a dress code, clearly set out in a sign posted at the entrance next to an officious and dour doorman. The requirements, which otherwise allowed for fairly relaxed apparel, included that would-be male patrons must wear closed-toed formal dress shoes. Almost all shoe-string budget backpackers on that island paradise arrived with nothing more than flip-flops, sandals, and sneakers. Blatantly sexist, the hotel policy allowed women to enter wearing sandals or even flip-flops. The doorman did not hesitate to turn away men without proper footwear.

The popularity of the drinks at Africa House led to a ritual established at the backpackers' guesthouse where I was staying. One of the backpackers was designated as the "keeper of the shoes", a pair of unadorned dark brown leather loafers that were about men's size eleven or twelve. No one recalled how these men's shoes had originally come to the guesthouse. On the appointed night, our group of partiers set off for the hotel, carrying the shoes, but stopping out of sight about a block away from the Africa House entrance.

We then commenced the following procedure: One of the male backpackers would pull on the leather shoes, hiding his own sneakers or sandals in a small daypack, under a light jacket, or in a purse carried by one of the female partiers. With proper footwear, that male backpacker would then saunter up to the hotel, pass the doorman at the entrance, and make his way upstairs to a specific second-floor room with a window opening to an unguarded side of the hotel. The window had no lock and was usually open to let in the cooling breeze. The leather shoes would be dropped through the window to the next male member of our party, who had made his way to that spot below a few minutes after the first backpacker had left the group for the hotel entrance. That second male backpacker would put on the brown loafers, enter the hotel past the doorman, and repeat the routine, dropping the shoes for the next guy who would show up below the window. The routine was repeated until all the backpackers had joined the gin and tonic party on the balcony.

Curiously, no one ever challenged our footwear once inside the hotel, or when we departed. The hotel bar staff were probably more interested in selling us drinks and getting tips than screening our footwear. And laughing at our shoes.

23. OPEN THE BAG, PLEASE

FROM ZANZIBAR AND Dar es Salaam, I headed towards Mombasa in Kenya just across the Tanzanian border. The first stop was Tanzania's second largest port, Tanga, and the bus pulled in at three a.m. in pitch darkness. Those of us not wishing to stay and visit Tanga were permitted to snooze on the bus until about five a.m., when we were kicked off for cleaning. I spent the next two pre-dawn hours on a nearby park bench, overlooking the port with its cargo-loading cranes. I had to wait to take a seven a.m. bus that would continue along the coast to the Kenyan border. However, it happened that the seven a.m. bus had broken down *en route* that day. I needed to wait in Tanga for the next bus not due to arrive until 2:30 in the afternoon.

Seven hours is a long time to watch clouds from a park bench.

After finding not much to do in Tanga, I boarded the 2:30 bus for onward travel. When the engine finally started and the vehicle lurched forward, a cardboard box belonging to another passenger fell from the rack above the seats. The carton dealt me a glancing blow on the head. I was not seriously hurt, but surprised when several of the passengers who saw the accident burst out laughing. It was funny to them, like the slap-stick humor of 1950s comedies featuring *Abbot and Costello* or the *Three Stooges*.

The seat beside me was occupied by Munir, who had Arabic features. Munir was immediately solicitous, reaching over to help with the fallen parcel and pushing it back up onto the rack.

"Are you all right?" Munir asked.

"Yeah, I'm fine," I answered, rubbing my temple where the corner of the box had grazed me.

"That is very unkind of them, the laughing," Munir continued. "But they don't know any better. They're Africans," he said, dismissively.

Munir spoke English in a soft tenor with clear enunciation and an almost-British accent. Although a citizen of Tanzania, obviously he did not consider himself "African." He was an Arab, traveling from his home on Zanzibar to visit his father in-law in Mombasa. Both the Muslim Arabs and the Christian blacks themselves referred to black persons in the country as "Africans." The two ethnic groups even maintained separate barber shops. Once, in Dar es Salaam, an Arab advised me to avoid getting a haircut, because (he said with disdain) the salon where I was headed had an "African barber."

Back in 1991, I did not believe any of the black people in Africa used, or felt the need to use, chemical or physical methods to straighten the tight curly, kinky hair that all black people are born with. Now I understand that even then, hot combs, perms, and hot irons were being used at home, especially on young women and girls, to flatten out the curls because few people could afford hair salons. Today, East African black society still struggles with its own ideals of beauty after its white British colonial past. In 2019, the Supreme Court of Kenya will decide whether Kenyan private schools have the right to determine and enforce dress codes dictating that black girls must have straight flat hair, no dreadlocks allowed.

The long and complicated bus ride to Mombasa was made tolerable by Munir. After small talk about where I was from and my travel plans, Munir offered me a handful of *khat* for chewing. Like *paan*, social khat chewing has been around for thousands of years. The fresh leaves and soft stems of the khat plant, *Catha edulis*, are chewed to release cathinone. Cathinone is an amphetamine that makes you feel excitement, loss of appetite, and euphoria. Munir carried a large bundle of the thin pliable foot-long purple stems, each with a top end sprouting a pair of soft green leaves. The plant is native to Ethiopia, Somalia, and the Arabian Peninsula. Khat is legal in several African countries where the plant is grown as a commercial crop. However, khat is a controlled drug in Canada, the US, and Britain.

My khat-chewing friend gave me all sorts of helpful insights to ease the border procedures. All I had to do in return was carry one of his many small bags for him, to ease his own trip past the officials. Munir was a small-time smuggler.

Halfway to the border, all passengers were ordered off the bus by Tanzanian police for a baggage check and individual interviews. I thought it strange to have a checkpoint here, on the side of the road without any building in sight, in addition to the inspections still to come at the actual border. After some perfunctory questions, I was allowed back onto the bus with the other passengers, and we continued the journey.

Forty minutes later, we were exiting Tanzania at Lunga Lunga. The bus passengers disembarked and were segregated by gender; women and their bags went through the customs check first, followed by the men. We each surrendered a currency declaration form. More rubber stamping followed over the next hour, and then we were directed to walk, carrying our bags, the short distance across a barren yard to the Kenya immigration building. Everyone queued up again for a health-card check and visa stamp, followed by another line up for a *preliminary* baggage check. We then queued up yet again for a *thorough* baggage check as the sun went down. The thorough baggage check took our group ninety minutes to process before we were all back on the bus.

Once on the highway inside Kenya, headed towards Mombasa, the bus was stopped twice more in the evening by Kenyan police officers. I was mystified by all these stops and delays until Munir leaned over and explained. Almost all the women on board were small-time smugglers too. Belatedly, I realized that except for five men including myself, all the other passengers were women with multiple bags. These women were smuggling simple personal luxuries such as cosmetics, bootleg music recordings, or name-brand shoes by Nike and Adidas. These goods were either more difficult to find in Kenya, or easier to counterfeit in Tanzania. At each of the previous stops, while I had been oblivious and baffled by the scrutiny, each of these women had been pressed for a small bribe by successive government officials. *Baksheesh*, fragrant grease, kickbacks, or hush money runs this part of the world. Apparently, backpackers were rare at this border crossing. These corrupt but good-natured officials had decided it was unfair to expect me to know the routine. They generously spared me from the requirement to contribute. I was also not smuggling anything from which they could reasonably expect a cut of the profit.

At the final police stop, the normality of bribes became apparent as all the passengers openly discussed who still needed to pay up their fair share for the two officers who had just detained the bus. About 150-200 Kenyan shillings per official was standard. Individuals passed forward their banknotes to achieve the required amount, and the bribes were handed to the two officers. People laughed on the bus as we drove off. Munir translated for me. One of the officers had been overheard complaining that it "wasn't fair" that he only got 150 shillings.

The city of Mombasa lies on an island set into the African coastline like a diamond in the prongs of a ring. The island is bordered on the east by the Indian Ocean. The prongs on the north and south of the island are formed from narrow inlets that curve towards each other in the west and connect, separating Mombasa from the mainland. As the bus pulled into a wharf at the end of the highway, everyone grabbed their numerous bags and dashed off the vehicle to catch the waiting ferry to Mombasa. Munir explained that they were attempting to outrun any Kenyan police. More Kenyan police might arrive at any moment to harass the incoming Tanzanians for more bribes.

As we reached the island and walked off the ferry, Munir insisted that I stay the night and experience Muslim generosity with his in-law's family on Mombasa. I accepted, grateful for a shower after two days on a bus, and a night on a proper mattress. I was welcomed to a clean and lovely home, with intricately patterned carpets covering the floor, rich Islamic tapestries adorning the walls, and pillows and cushions everywhere in lieu of chairs. The hour was late, and after showering, we went straight to bed. In the morning, I was treated to a breakfast of eggs, fried potatoes in a sour sauce, and sweet coconut rice cakes. I talked with Munir and his father-in-law about Mombasa's story, and the modern challenges faced by the islanders. Munir's father-in-law was concerned that the local politicians were becoming too cozy with organized crime.

The history of Mombasa is somewhat similar to that of Zanzibar. Both were important bases for Arab traders plying their goods on Indian Ocean trade routes. Mombasa's main exports were ivory, sesame seeds, millet (a grain), and coconuts. The Portuguese arrived and took the city by force, building their massive Fort Jesus in 1593. The Portuguese soldiers at Fort Jesus were slaughtered by the island's Arab population on several occasions, but Mombasa remained under Portuguese rule until 1698, when the Arabs under the Sultanate of Oman took the fort by siege. Following tussles between Oman, Portugal, and Britain, the city came to be controlled by the powerful British East Africa Company in 1897.

That chartered Company declared Mombasa to be the capital city of Kenya. Then the company built the Uganda Railway to export products from Africa's interior. Mombasa became the sea terminal of the railway.

Nairobi was at the geographical halfway point between Kampala in Uganda and Mombasa on the coast. Over time, Nairobi grew from an uninhabited swamp to an important supply depot for the railway. The Company moved the capital from Mombasa to Nairobi in 1905. Mombasa remained part of the British Kenya Colony, until it became a city of the independent Republic of Kenya in 1964.

The Mombasa that I discovered was full of casinos, bars, and mosques, clearly still more Arabic than African. It was a port city catering to some very wealthy jetsetters. It was easy to find good food. I enjoyed bananas, mangoes, coffee and muffins, beer, chicken, potato chips, roasted cashews, and chocolate bars. After visiting Fort Jesus, I sought refreshment at a pub and struck up a conversation with a sixty-year old Indian man. He was proud of his longevity. Like his father and grandfather, this man had spent his entire life in Mombasa. He bought me a beer and stressed that it was important to be careful in that city, to not get involved, and to avoid discussing politics. He echoed the words of Munir's father-in-law that "Mombasa is finished." He predicted the future of the city held only escalating crime and a colder, uncaring society. I think it is common in every country for the older generation to believe that the best days are all in the past.

24. A WALK IN THE PARK

AFTER LEAVING MOMBASA, I lingered a few days in Nairobi to acquire a visa to enter Egypt on my next flight. Then I headed northwest to visit Kenya's Hell's Gate National Park. For accommodations, I stayed a few kilometres away at a place called Fisherman's Camp on the shores of Lake Naivasha. The private campground had an area for tents, several cottages with rooms for rent, and a common building with food for sale. I opted for a bed in one of the cottages.

I shared a dinner of canned beans, bananas, tomatoes, bread, oranges, and beer with a group of backpackers. We swapped travel advice and anecdotes, laughing for hours. Night had fallen by the time we left the common building. We started on the short walk along the lakeshore, back to the cottages at the far end of the campground. Everyone was excited, hoping to meet Huey, one of the resident hippopotamuses in Lake Naivasha. Huey had been making a habit of coming out of the water to wander the grassy areas early, around eight or nine p.m., rather than later with the other hippos which generally came out around two or three a.m. at night.

In the pitch darkness, we proceeded carefully following somebody's weak flashlight with a failing battery, pointed ahead and at the ground before us. Sure enough, the flashlight soon illuminated a blackness in front that was subtly different from the darkness on either side. It was the hide of a hippopotamus, standing directly across our path. It was huge. One of the girls in our party, Tracy, had an irresistible urge to pet Huey. We had to physically bat her hands away from touching the animal. Contrary to cartoonish depictions of lovable hippos, these animals are highly aggressive and dangerous.

    I chose the next morning to leave for a visit to Hell's Gate Park. I took leave of my senses that morning as well. Fisherman's Camp was seven kilometres away from Elsa Gate at the Hell's Gate Park entrance. It would cost 200 Kenyan shillings, or about nine Canadian dollars, for a cab to take me there. These were the days before cell phones, and I would first need to locate a landline telephone whose owner would allow me to use it to call a cab. If I somehow managed to hail a cab from the remoteness of Fisherman's Camp, I wasn't sure how I could arrange for one to pick me up at the park gate several hours later. Nor did I know how long I would want to stay exploring inside the park before returning for a pre-arranged pickup time at the gate.

    Because of these uncertainties, and to save myself the cost of transportation, I decided to start walking and secure a ride by hitch-hiking. *How hard could it be?* I set off with some bottled water, half a loaf of bread, and some cookies.

    The highway curved east along the southern shore of Lake Naivasha. Then it turned south through a small Maasai village before continuing east. I diligently stuck out my thumb at every passing truck, matutu, and car, but had even less luck than on Fiji. Nobody stopped. After the first five kilometres, I resigned myself to walking all the way to park gate.

    It took me two hours, and some back-tracking along nondescript roads without signage, to reach Elsa Gate by an unassuming country lane branching off the main highway. I chatted briefly with the park rangers stationed there. They provided me with information about the trail conditions, and then I set off into the national park itself.

First, I walked past Fischer's tower, a dramatic conical volcanic plug some twenty-five meters high. It was named after a German explorer who came upon it in 1882, even though the local Maasai no doubt knew of the landmark a thousand years earlier. From there, I walked along a dirt path in the centre of a wide, flat green valley bounded by red sandstone cliffs on either side. There was an abundance of wildlife. Hartebeest, gazelle, impala, zebra, and ostrich all fled behind the horizon almost as soon as I spotted them through my binoculars. Today, most visitors rent bicycles at the park entrance for this stretch of the trail, but no such rental facilities existed in 1991. The government of Kenya had established the park a mere seven years before the time of my visit.

Seven kilometres later, I arrived at Hell's Gate Gorge. The entrance to the gorge is a claustrophobic, almost tunnel-like gap between cliff walls eroded by water into layered shelves. It is part of the Great Rift Valley that bisects Kenya from north to south. The rift is the result of the Somali Plate in the east pulling away from the main Africa Plate in the west, creating a gap or valley as the chunk of land between the two separating tectonic plates drops into the rift. Like many before me, I clambered through the narrow opening and descended for an hour along the gorge. The route follows a dry riverbed, with shallow pools remaining in a few places during the dry season.

Along the gradually widening gorge, I saw the occasional tracks in the mud left by my old friend the Cape buffalo. Fortunately, no buffalo came within sight. It was probably not a good idea to be there alone without a hired guide, anyway, in an area prone to flash floods. I had already been caught in one unexpected rainstorm during the dry season.

At length, the few traces of water disappeared entirely, and the gorge walls became chalky, collapsing in rubble at spots. The park rangers had told me there were hot springs two hours beyond Hell's Gate, but by 3:15 p.m. I had finished my loaf of bread, snacks, and water. It was time to head back to the top of the gorge in order to reach Elsa Gate by closing time at six p.m.

The sun went down as I continued walking from Elsa Gate to Fisherman's Camp. My thumb was out, but not a single passing vehicle pulled over to offer me a lift, even though I was by now quite willing to pay. I was useless at hitch-hiking without Mariana. It was lucky that I had been able to purchase additional bottled water from the park rangers.

By the time I sat down on my bed at Fisherman's Camp, I had walked a distance of thirty-eight kilometres. My feet and legs would be sore and aching for three days. Hitch-hiking had completely lost its appeal.

25. DESERT RICHES

THERE ARE MANY times on extended backpack travel when you get absolutely fed up. This was one of those times. I was standing on the sandy shore of a lake, just outside the tiny village of Kalokol in the remote northwestern corner of Kenya. I glared at the little boy in front of me. I had just asked him to point, left or right, to indicate which way it was to a fishing lodge I had read about. But he wanted a payment first.

Kalokol was at the end of the route served by matutus. From Naivasha, I had travelled steadily north, visiting the flamingoes at Lake Elmentaita, exploring up the rim of the Menengai Crater, and then continuing through increasingly arid landscape beyond Kitale and Lodwar. The matutu rides were riveting. The drivers speed on through country highways past dusk without headlights, and into the night. Occasionally, when rounding a bend or spying an oncoming vehicle in the distance with supernatural night vision, my driver would flick his headlights on and off, twice. The oncoming driver would do the same in acknowledgement. The explanation I was given was that matutu drivers used their headlamps only when absolutely necessary, to delay the expense of buying replacement bulbs for as long as possible.

I arrived in Kalokol in the dark of night, but somehow a tout found me anyway to guide me to a guesthouse and receive a tip. The only place for visitors to stay overnight was a gated compound with half a dozen single-room huts. The huts had corrugated metal walls. Each hut had a bed, a night stand with a lamp, and a small dresser. There was a separate building with shared washroom facilities. The next day, there appeared to be only one place in town where you could buy a meal. There was only one option on the lunch menu: a fish, pan-fried whole with head and tail, served on a plate with a bottle of Coke. No sauce, no rice, no French fries, no veggies. Kalokol was little more than a cluster of buildings around a church and a primary school, and so I was thankful I didn't have to go catch my lunch.

To the east of Kalokol is Lake Turkana, the world's largest alkaline desert lake. The lake is long and narrow, with its ends on a north-south axis. Stretching into the distance north and west of Kalokol is a pitiless expanse of orange sand and scraggly shrubs. Living in the Turkana desert are the nomadic goat-herding Turkana people, their lifestyle almost unchanged by the modern world. They raise camels and weave baskets for cash sales. The Turkana number about 900,000 souls, slightly greater than the more well-known Maasai tribes in the south.

I had left the Kalokol guesthouse with my backpack. My goal that afternoon was to walk to the Lake Turkana Fishing Lodge. The lodge had a restaurant and even an outdoor swimming pool. My travel guidebook had a map showing that the lodge was within walking distance, but due to the small scale of the map, it was hard to tell whether the lodge was north or south of Kalokol where I had spent the night. I deduced that it was simply a matter of following the only road east out of town until I came to the shore of the lake, and then turning ninety degrees to follow the shoreline road until reaching the hotel. There was no Google Maps back then, and even today I would be surprised if there were wireless service in that region. I was happy at first when a boy of perhaps twelve years fortuitously appeared as I approached the lakeshore.

Now, he wanted a few Kenyan shillings before telling me whether I needed to turn and walk north or south.

Today, thirty years later, I wish I had had more compassion and generosity for that youngster. At the time, however, I had already endured weeks of African touts seeking tips for every imaginable "service," wanted or not. I turned abruptly on my heel in disgust and walked away from the boy, picking a direction at random. I would soon discover whether my choice was correct, either by arriving at the lodge or by doubling back in twenty minutes or so to proceed in the opposite direction.

After I left that boy, I saw no one and no sign of human presence except for the road. I walked doggedly south in silence with the lake to my left, fuming. The shore birds that occasionally flittered past were my only company.

The Turkana area was active with VSOs, professionals recruited by the international charity Voluntary Service Overseas. VSOs live with impoverished local populations of developing countries and work to improve their lives. As luck would have it, I soon heard the sound of a vehicle engine and spinning wheels. Out on Ferguson Gulf on the western shore of the lake, a couple of German VSOs had ventured too far towards the water in their Land Rover. The car was stuck in the soft mud of the wide shore. I approached, dropping my pack onto the sand. I joined one man pushing the sunken vehicle from the rear, while the other VSO worked the accelerator pedal to rock the car free.

Adding my efforts made the difference, and with a few heaves, we managed to unstick the car. The grateful Germans offered me a ride. Coincidentally, the VSOs had also been headed to the Lake Turkana Fishing Lodge. As the miles rolled by in the Land Rover, I realized that I had been sadly mistaken to think the lodge was within easy walking distance of Kalokol. My small-scale map of the region appeared to show the lodge a few kilometres away from the village. While this was the true distance as the crow flies, the map didn't show enough detail to reveal that the lodge sat at the end of a long thin curved peninsula creating Ferguson's Bay. A long and narrow sliver of water lay between the lodge and Kalokol. Without a boat, you reach the lodge from Kalokol by driving south almost ten kilometres to the base of the peninsula, making a hair-pin turn and then driving north ten kilometres to the tip of the peninsula. If I had not encountered the Germans, I might have been walking all day to discover I was totally lost at sundown, miles away from help or shelter.

When we reached the fishing lodge, the Germans continued to show their appreciation by buying me beer. The only other patrons at the bar were three Spaniards who spoke perfect English. The Spaniards were Christian missionaries, also working to help the Turkana people. One of the Spaniards was a videographer. The group was filming a video to showcase their charitable activities and solicit donations back home in Europe. Paco, their leader, spontaneously offered me room and board for a few days with his group, if I were willing to contribute in manual labor. After enjoying the beer, food, showers, and a deliciously cool pool at the lodge that night, I departed the next day with Paco and his companions to the village of Lowarengak.

When most people think of Kenya, they are probably not imagining a desert. However, the northern half of Kenya is bone dry for ten months of the year. I was astounded that any humans could survive that land of orange sand and low thorny bushes. When the rains do come, they can be torrential, creating instant rivers that carve new slopes into the bare dirt landscape. However, there are stretches of many years where little if any rain falls. During a drought, vegetation shrivels up, the animals that eat it die off, and the people who depend on the animals soon follow.

The villages at Kalokol, Lodwar, and Lowarengak all originated as famine relief camps in the 1920s and 1960s. Through these camps, the Kenyan government saved thousands of Turkana families after their goat and camel herds had died of starvation during prolonged droughts. The problem was that, after drought conditions eased, generations of Turkana people had grown up in the camps with a lifestyle of dependency on government handouts. Their livestock was gone, and the new generations had no desert survival skills. Forcing these Turkana people out of the camps back into the desert would have been sending them to their deaths. Eventually, the Kenyan government's solution was to set up programs to provide replacement animals while phasing out food handouts. It seemed harsh, but I suppose that before the government stepped in during the 1920s, the Turkana families simply died off with their livestock during periodic droughts over the centuries.

I spent five days with the Spaniards, loading hundred-litre steel drums onto trucks to store and transport drinking water, digging a six-meter hole for a septic tank, and just tagging along in a speeding Land Rover as the missionaries filmed their documentary in various locations. Meal times were excellent opportunities for me to improve my Spanish (*Me passas la leche por favor?*). The base of the Spanish operation was a residential complex in Lowarengak. We used a manual pump in the town to obtain water from a well. The water pump was simple to operate until fatigue set in after five minutes of continuous effort pumping.

International aid had provided Lowarengak a solar-powered water pump, but the solar panels had been vandalized. It was an example of how foreign aid was stymied by local culture and practices. Prior to the installation of the solar-powered pump, Lowarengak received water deliveries by truck, because of the laborious and inefficient pumping required at the well. When the solar pump was installed, the individuals who had delivered water by truck lost their jobs. To regain employment, these delivery men smashed the solar panels. They had been destroying replacement panels ever since. It was clearly targeted vandalism, because other solar panels that powered the refrigerator for vaccines in the Lowarengak pharmacy were left untouched.

On the shore of Lake Turkana, we passed a large, modern-looking but abandoned fish-processing plant. It was yet another example of international aid gone sideways. The population of tilapia and Nile perch in Lake Turkana is large enough for commercial export. The story I was told was that, in the 1970s, the Norwegian government provided twenty-two million US dollars to build the fish-processing plant to generate local employment. At first, the plant had difficulty attracting local laborers. The Turkana nomads had no history or practice of fishing or eating fish. Another challenge was that, after Turkana workers had been lured into training and employment, many of these employees did not bother to return to the fish plant after payday. Turkana people were not accustomed to stable, predictable and regular working hours for long-term employment and savings. In their thinking, the Turkana fish-plant workers already had money in their pockets after their first paycheck. They had no need to return to work until those funds ran out days or even weeks later.

Thirty years after my visit, the world has continued to be unkind to the Turkana people. Droughts have continued to force more families out of the desert into a lifestyle dependent on fishing at the lake. Today, Kalokol is a centre of commercial gill-net fisheries using small wooden boats. New arrivals from the desert learn fishing from Turkana families already settled. The villagers have organized themselves into groups to repair boats, make sails, and prepare catches for transport by truck to distant markets.

Despite this adaptation, the Turkana people are under increasing threats. As families migrate from the desert to the lakeshore, more and more of the young men are acquiring guns and adopting a lifestyle supported by raiding the fishing communities. Why fish when you can just take someone else's fish? Meanwhile, Kenya's neighbour Ethiopia is constructing a dam upstream. The dam will severely reduce Lake Turkana water levels, and correspondingly, its fish populations.

The aid projects of the Spanish missionaries with whom I spent my time were modest and pragmatic. Projects included a nutritional program at the local school. The missionaries also operated a mobile vaccination clinic to prevent polio, tuberculosis, diphtheria, tetanus, and measles. The Spanish group included a registered nurse, who gave talks and injected vaccines at the school and villages. This was not as easy as I would have thought for a free medical service. It was exceedingly difficult to convince the local nomads to accept "medicine" through a needle in the arm, or to allow their children to be pricked, when they were not already sick. Most Turkana individuals would come looking for a vaccination only after they were experiencing advanced symptoms of an infection. The Turkana wise men, or medicine men, also castigated their people for believing the quackery of these foreign western doctors.

One morning, our group of do-gooders prepared for an overnight visit to film a Turkana family in its natural temporary homestead. There were eight of us travelling in two Land Rovers: four missionaries, a videographer, a nurse, an interpreter, and myself. The Land Rovers sped through hours of road-free desert, hauntingly beautiful from the comfort of a car. At last, we arrived at a cluster of three dome-shaped huts made of branches and twigs. It was home base for a Turkana man, his wife, and two daughters. Each dome hut was about five feet high and perhaps seven feet in diameter. Each hut had an opening to crouch through and no door. Inside the huts, the only furnishings were a few gourds that had been hollowed out to serve as water jugs or cups, all fitted with animal hide straps to hang from the hut walls. Twenty paces away from the huts, there was an enclosure created by dragging whole dried scrub bushes loose by the roots and piling them up to form a low fence. A herd of some thirty goats was corralled inside.

The landscape looked painfully dry. Seasonal rains, never generous, were now overdue by months. The two Turkana girls were sprawled on a tanned leather carpet on the bare ground, playing with what looked like an antelope horn. The children wore only leather wraps and were barefoot. Their body odour was the product of weeks or months without a bath, and nauseating.

Two girls at their homestead in the Turkana desert of Kenya.

It was impossible to tell the age of the Turkana head man. He looked old and frail, with twigs for legs, but he might have seen no more than forty years in that harsh environment. His torso was wrapped in a traditional striped, home-spun rectangular blanket. His head was covered by a hat resembling a woven basket worn upside down. Under one arm, he carried a long staff to prod livestock. In his hand was a curious object that turned out to be a stool to avoid sitting directly on the hot desert sand. The stool, or *ekicholong*, looked like an inverted coffee cup with a miniature skateboard affixed to the bottom of the cup to provide a sitting surface. I was told that you won't find any respectable grown male Turkana without his ekicholong.

Life for the Turkana people is spent surviving on the very little afforded by their environment. Turkana men take out their goats to find fresh grazing areas in the day. Turkana women stay at the huts to milk camels and make cheese or walk up to two hours away for water supplies. It was not possible to live near the water source permanently, because of the constant need to find fresh areas for the goats and camels to graze. Livestock rustling was rampant. This Turkana man had traded many camels and goats to obtain a rifle for protection against thieves.

I would be spending the night with the Spaniards sleeping under the stars next to the homestead. There were no mosquitoes or winds, and the temperature was pleasant. The land was silent except for the occasional bleat of a goat or a bird chirping. At dusk, the Spaniards broke out food and flashlights from the vehicles for a sumptuous picnic dinner. I commented that it seemed tactless to show such abundance in full view of the destitute Turkana family we were visiting. Paco overheard and patronizingly rebuked me.

"That is a very western-centric viewpoint," Paco admonished. "These are people from an entirely different culture. They see life very differently and consider themselves equal in wealth to us because they have freedom, goats, camels, and simplicity. You are showing your prejudices by assuming they would want anything like your materialistic lifestyle," he concluded.

The Turkana people speak the Turkana language, indigenous to this area of the Rift Valley. A local non-Turkana Kenyan woman had accompanied our group to act as an interpreter. Through her, Paco offered his compliments to the Turkana man. Paco said the head man must have worked hard to accumulate such riches, with so many goats in his herd and camels to carry him as far as Nairobi.

The Turkana man's eyes widened. His reply was sharp and obviously irritated. The Kenyan translator provided the Turkana man's response to Paco in Spanish that I didn't understand, but even in the lantern light, I could see Paco's complexion darken. Later, one of the other Spaniards in our group explained that the Turkana man was highly insulted. He had told Paco, "How dare you come with your Land Rovers and your cameras and your fine clothes, and suggest that I, a poor man trapped in the desert, have anything resembling wealth? Yes, my camels can get you to Nairobi, but only a fool would not take a Land Rover instead." The rest of the conversation had revolved around the Turkana man's requests to Paco, making repeated entreaties for guns, pots, knives, lighters, and rope.

26. PEACHES AND PEBBLES

I HAD BEEN TRAVELLING for nine months now. Just what was I going to do with my life when this walk-about ended? Not only would the money run out, I was growing weary of being an observer without purpose, no matter how spectacular or exotic the world around me.

Again, I thought about starting a new life with Mariana in Spain. I reread the letter from her that I had retrieved from *poste restante* in Nairobi. I missed the slight lisp in her voice and her infectious laugh. The way she'd throw me a look of mischief, then with a toss of her hair, dare me to join her in some new or risky venture. I did not know much about Spain, but I liked the idea of living with Mariana there. And there was the appeal of staying in a European country with a hot dry climate and a long colorful history.

Perhaps, using my Spanish contacts from the Turkana, I could find work with a non-profit conservation project? My missionary friends in Kenya had also given me the contact information for a desert-irrigation technology company in Spain.

With increasing frequency, I was hit by spells of worry, pondering career directions or lack thereof. When not thinking about Mariana and Spain, I was brain-storming. Maybe I could have a future as a salesman for a pharmaceutical or biotechnology company. Maybe I should try science journalism. Maybe I could train to be a fireman. But I was passionate about none of these options. More likely I would simply run out of savings and be forced to apply for a McJob, flipping burgers. I was looking for the perfect career that would hold my interest for my entire life and pay well too.

I never dreamed that I would still be searching for that perfect job almost thirty years later, during my third "career."

For now, I was in Cairo. The City of Cairo is referred to by the locals as "Egypt." The desert looked bleak and desolate from the airplane window before landing, but Cairo? It was like New York. Home to millions of people, Cairo was a major concrete jungle with shopping at bargain-basement prices. Of course, there was precious little signage in English and the baking sun at thirty-three degrees Celsius gave me headaches. I quickly spent money on gauze-thin clothing, new sandals, and liquids. My favourite drinks were refreshing pureed mango smoothies that cost one Egyptian pound a glass (about thirty Canadian cents), available from roadside push-cart vendors.

As with every country I had visited since leaving Thailand, the local inhabitants were curious about me. "Where you from? Japan? Hong Kong? Philippines?"

I found an inexpensive hotel in the heart of old Cairo. In the lobby, there was another backpacker checking out the same day I checked in, and we discovered we were kindred spirits. He was headed to East Africa. I told him what to expect from my experiences, while he described his adventures in Egypt. At the end of our hours-long conversation, I unburdened myself of my heavy industrial-strength mosquito net. He had not been able to buy one despite searching high and low in Cairo. I sold him mine to raise some cash and lighten my load, reckoning that I had only a few short weeks in Egypt before continuing to mosquito-free Europe. That was my first mistake.

In Egypt, the mosquitoes were fierce and incredibly tenacious. Bereft of my mosquito net, I spent the nights in Cairo sweating profusely under a sheet pulled up over my face to block the insects, with only my mouth exposed to breathe. I woke frequently to fend off the creatures trying to sink their needle noses into my lips, or to spit out crunchy insect parts. Often, I resorted to daytime naps to make up for the sleep deprivation.

One of the greatest of humanity's ancient civilizations, the Egypt of the pharoahs owed much of its success to an accident of geography. The Nile River flows from south to north, originating from tributaries deep inside the African continent and emptying through a delta at Cairo. The prevailing winds blow in the opposite direction, from north to south. Boat transportation along the linear nation of ancient Egypt was easy: put up a sail and the wind blew you south on the Nile; take down your sail and the river current carried you back north to Cairo. Pharoah's empire was bordered in the north by the Mediterranean Sea. His lands were protected from invading armies on east, west, and south by vast expanses of sand-dune desert. Agricultural food production was assured by the rich river-delta soils that were recharged every year between June and September when the Nile flooded over its banks.

With safety from invaders and reliable supplies of food and water, the dynasties of the pharoahs were able to thrive. For over two thousand years, the Egyptians developed their culture, art, and technology without fear of barbarian attacks. Narmer was the first pharoah to unite Upper and Lower Egypt at about 3,100 BCE. The parade of pharoahs continued for over three thousand years, even after the Egyptian army was defeated by the Persians in 525 BCE. Then Alexander the Great of Macedonia (modern Greece) arrived in 331 BCE. However, instead of being feared as another conqueror, Alexander was welcomed by the Egyptians for liberating them from the Persians.

Alexander founded the city of Alexandria on the Mediterranean coast as his new capital of Egypt, replacing the old capital at Memphis. Alexandria lies 200 kilometres northwest of Cairo. When Alexander died only two years later, one of his military generals, a Greek fellow by the name of Ptolemy, became the next pharoah and ruled Egypt from Alexandria. Ptolemy started a dynasty, and the last pharoah whose title held any power in Egypt was his descendent, Cleopatra VII.

Cleopatra first ruled jointly with her father, Ptolemy number twelve. When Ptolemy XII died in 51 BCE, eighteen-year-old Cleopatra was married to her twelve-year-old brother, Ptolemy XIII, to rule Egypt with him jointly. She soon removed her little brother's name from all official documents to rule the kingdom on her own. With their Greek lineage, all the Ptolemy children were educated in the Greek language. However, Cleopatra also spoke native Egyptian, Ethiopian, Hebrew, Arabic, and four more ancient languages that no longer exist. She confidently conducted business with diplomats from other countries without translators, and then without bothering to listen to any of her Egyptian counselors. Eventually, her chief counselor Pothinus had had enough. He carried out a coup in 48 BCE. Pothinus put little brother Ptolemy XIII on the throne, thinking the teenage boy would be easy to control. Cleopatra went into hiding in southern Egypt.

The power of Rome arrived in Alexandria that same year with the coming of Julius Caesar himself. Caesar had just defeated Pompey the Great in the Roman civil war, at the Battle of Pharsalus. After the battle, Pompey fled to Alexandria. Caesar went after him. When Pompey arrived in Alexandria, he was assassinated by Ptolemy XIII. But when Ptolemy learned that Caesar was coming next with his army, Ptolemy ran away from the city before Caesar arrived. Caesar's army tracked down Ptolemy XIII hiding in the fortress at Pelusium, to drag him back to Alexandria for judgment.

Cleopatra was still in exile, but she saw a chance to regain power through Caesar. She needed a way to talk to Caesar, who was deep inside the palace at Alexandria. If she tried to walk in, she would likely be stopped by opposing Egyptians loyal to Ptolemy XIII, or by the Roman army. Cleopatra had herself rolled up in a luxurious carpet, to be presented to Caesar as a gift. Hidden inside the carpet, she was carried by co-conspirators straight through enemy lines into the throne room. When the carpet was unrolled, Cleopatra picked herself up off the floor and presented herself to Caesar.

Caesar and Cleopatra were drawn to each other instantly. Caesar was *the* world power. Cleopatra was twenty-two years old, smart, persuasive, and smokin' hot. By the time Ptolemy XIII arrived in Alexandria the next day to discover his fate, Caesar and Cleopatra had already transformed into the two-backed beast, panting in the royal bed. Cleopatra once again became Pharoah of Egypt, while Caesar was the Emperor in Rome. When Cleopatra died in 30 BCE, the once great kingdom of Egypt became a province of Rome.

Over the span of three millennia, the pharaohs of Egypt gave the world jaw-dropping pyramids, temples, tombs, monuments and the fantastical Book of the Dead. When the mosquitoes relented at daybreak, I went to eat some breakfast from a market stall. Then I retreated to my hotel room to plan a route to the historic sites scattered down the length of the Nile.

The Cairo hotel was bare bones. It came with lots of flies and mosquitoes, but often no running water. Guests were asked to use water stored in plastic bottles provided in the bathroom, clearly marked "not for drinking." The containers were re-filled from commercial bottled-water products. On the plus side, I befriended a seasoned French traveler, Thierry, staying at the same hotel.

Thierry had a tall straight nose, light grey eyes, and close-cropped curly brown hair. He was always carrying a small messenger bag of worn brown leather with its strap over one shoulder.

Thierry was amazing. He knew exactly when the shared minivan drivers were overcharging us; the price the locals paid for a cup of tea; when to ignore the touts demanding an entrance fee to free public sites; and when it was better to pay that fee instead of fighting the hassle that would follow if we did not. Thierry was mystifyingly certain that taxis and buses would reach our intended destination and was always proven correct. And he knew exactly the right moment to tell a tout to leave us, using choice French expressions that I am sure were not polite.

With Thierry, I went to visit the iconic Pyramids of Giza on the edge of Cairo. You could take a bus from downtown right to the admission gates on the Giza plateau. The oldest and largest pyramid, rising 481 feet, was completed by Pharoah Khufu (or his Greek name of Cheops) around 2560 BCE. This was followed by the successively smaller pyramids of pharaohs who came after: Khafre who completed his monument around 2530 BCE, and Menkaure who completed his around 2510 BCE. The great pyramids were constructed as burial chambers. There are records that Khufu needed to clear away the tombs and burial complexes of previous Egyptian kings from the plateau before he could build his first gargantuan pyramid.

Thierry navigated our transportation to Giza. We arrived after 11 a.m. under a pitiless sun. Thierry restricted us to two reasonably priced drinks apiece. He was schooling me in the ways of the shoe-string budget traveler who needed to ration a finite amount of cash in order to sustain an extended period of travel.

We visited the musty room inside the Pyramid of Khufu that was open to the public. The entrance was on the north side, above ground. There was only one room, which you accessed through a sloping tunnel with a low ceiling that forced you to crouch. The tunnel was just wide enough for two people to pass side by side. Lit only by dim bare light bulbs spaced twenty feet apart, the shaft was not recommended for the claustrophobic. There was nothing in the room except an empty stone sarcophagus. All the burial items recovered in modern times were on display elsewhere at museums in other countries. Thierry and I were lucky. Only about a dozen other tourists were squeezing into the room at the same time as us. The ancient dark and dank chamber reeked from the perspiration of modern visitors.

Leaving the burial chamber, we wandered at leisure among the excavated *mastabas* in cemeteries arrayed east and west of Khufu's pyramid. A *mastaba* is a stone tomb structure for royalty and wealthy individuals. We then trekked counter-clockwise around the historic complex to visit the three small queen's pyramids south of Menkaure's pyramid. The queens' pyramids were for the mother or wives of Pharoah. Next, like thousands before us, we stopped to photograph and ponder the mystery of the Sphinx.

The giant stone carving known as the Sphinx lies about half a kilometre east of the pyramid of Khafre. The statue is 260 feet long, with its head reaching up 65 feet. Having the reclining body and front paws of a lion and the head of a pharoah, the statue resembles the mythical female monster who tries to stump the heroes in Greek legends with riddles. However, the Egyptian Great Sphinx is itself a riddle. Even today, scholars debate when the Great Sphinx was built, for what purpose, and for whom. There is no clue what it was called before European explorers in the 1700s dubbed it "the Sphinx." Someone carved it from the limestone bedrock of Giza, then it got covered by desert sand up to its shoulders, and then it was mostly forgotten. It was not until 1817 that an Italian explorer, Giovanni Caviglia, led an expedition to dig out the Sphinx.

At about two o'clock in the afternoon, Thierry advised it was best to leave the over-heating desert plateau. He said I could return a few hours later if I wanted to watch the sun setting over the pyramids. While Thierry did depart from Giza, I elected to stay. I did not want to pay the entrance fee of ten Egyptian pounds again. That was my second mistake.

I toughed it out for two more hours in the heat, then threw economy to the winds and spent over twenty Egyptian pounds on life-preserving fluids. I imagine I was in the early stages of heat stroke.

Armed with another liter of purchased drinking water, I returned to the shade of the giant stone slabs on the east side of Khufu's pyramid. Each rectangular stone block is shockingly huge. A block lying on its side at the base of the pyramid is about five feet high. It took some effort to pull myself up by the arms, starting with the upper edge of a block just under my armpits. I climbed only two more levels before deciding it was too hot and dangerous to go higher. As well as the distance from the ground, the sandstone blocks became progressively more uneven and fractured with each level up. I retreated down to the first level.

To make me feel even more pathetic while I was trying to move as little as possible in the heat, staying in the shade, a group of six young boys was playing soccer next to the pyramid to pass the time. I suppose their parents were on a camel ride in the desert or touring a burial chamber. The boys appeared to be Muslim locals, all about ten to twelve years old. They energetically chased the ball in long-sleeved shirts, long pants, and jackets. After twenty minutes, one of them finally got a little warm. He removed his jacket, tossing it to the ground near me on one side of the field of play.

There was a little girl watching me, next to her mother. They were also camped in the shade a few feet away. I surmised that they were related to one or more of the soccer boys. The girl and her mother had a cooler full of picnic supplies. The girl kept watching me, then said something to her mother. The mother nodded. The little girl, maybe nine years old, reached into the cooler. She pulled out a couple of items, and then shyly approached me with a smile. Without a word, she held out two peaches.

I gratefully accepted her offering. She giggled and ran back to her mother. I called a thank you to her mother as well. Once again, I had received unlooked-for generosity from strangers. The peaches were juicy and delicious.

When at last the sun was tolerably low in the sky, I resumed wandering the vast site to get some photos in the more interesting lighting conditions. I slogged far out into the shifting dunes on foot. My camera lens captured a group of tourists galloping on horseback, the back-lit dust plume from their passage fanning out dramatically behind them. In another scene, a couple of tourists and their guide on camels stopped to gaze and marvel at the pyramids from a vantage point where the queens' pyramids were arrayed in a line with the three giant pyramids looming behind.

Rather than being surrounded by desert, the pyramids would have sat in the middle of urban sprawl when they were being built. The first clue to this came when an American tourist was thrown from her horse in 1990 while galloping in the Giza dunes, just a year before I arrived. The horse had tripped over a low mud-brick wall buried in the sand. In the years following my visit, excavations revealed the Lost City of Giza. These were the buildings that housed and fed thousands of laborers and craftsmen who built the pyramids, as well as the grocers, tailors, and shopkeepers needed to support them. The great pyramids were built by paid laborers, not slaves as many people nowadays believe.

Back in 1991, the giant stone pyramids were still isolated in a sea of sand. The strangest sight was the low stone wall preventing the desert from spilling out into the urban sprawl of modern Cairo at the entry gate to the Giza historic site. It was this desert that allowed an aggressive army of touts to push camel and horseback rides on tourists. The animals could help to cover the lengthy distances between points of interest while exposed to the scorching sun or provide thrill rides in the desert with the pyramids as a gorgeous backdrop.

"Hello! Where you from? Want a camel ride? Know how much? Later if you change your mind?" This litany was repeated by every tout I encountered. Soon, I was sure I was being targeted by the same touts over and over. The aggressiveness of the Giza touts is legendary. Many tourists report verbal abuse from these touts when their services are turned down.

After declining a camel ride for the umpteenth time from yet another tout, a youth of perhaps seventeen, I relaxed in the shade of Khafre's pyramid to wait until sunset. With my photographer's itch almost sated, I struck up a conversation with a Caucasian Briton named Tim who was also travelling solo. We traded opinions of the various sites at Giza, which we had each just visited independently. The tout who had tried to sell me a camel ride remained a few meters away with his animal, unable to convince any other tourist to engage his services. In his boredom, or perhaps frustration, the tout picked up a handful of pebbles and began tossing them one by one at his tethered camel.

I was deep in conversation with Tim when I felt a pebble hit my shoulder. I looked in the direction of the tout just as another stone caught me on the side of the head. I was astonished, for indeed, the tout was now tossing his pebbles at me. Tim reacted at the same time I did.

"Hey!" I yelled.

"What the hell are you doing?" Tim said.

The Egyptian youth pointedly addressed Tim, ignoring eye contact with me. "It's okay. He's Japanese," he replied. "They don't mind stones."

I was flabbergasted. Tim was more articulate. "What are you talking about?" he demanded, angrily.

The tout continued casually tossing stones in my direction, although they were now only landing at my feet. "Don't worry, I won't hurt him," he assured Tim. "It's okay for Japanese; they don't complain. But not Europeans. You can't throw stones at Europeans," he said.

"I'm actually from Canada," I clarified. Stupidly.

"Are you really saying it's okay to throw stones at people?" Tim said, incensed.

"Alright, I'll stop if he's from Canada," the tout said. He shrugged, and added, "I didn't throw hard, anyway," as if that were enough to excuse his actions.

Clearly not the least bit embarrassed or defensive, the Egyptian youth stayed put. He turned his attention back to tossing pebbles at his camel.

27. LITTERING THE NILE

And on the pedestal these words appear:
'My name is Ozymandias, king of kings:
Look on my works, ye Mighty, and despair!'

"Ozymandias" by Percy Shelley

OVER 1,100 KILOMETRES south of Cairo lies another UNESCO World Heritage site: the temple of Abu Simbel built around 1250 BCE by Pharaoh Ramses II. Ramses had stoneworkers carve four gigantic seated statues of his own magnificent self. Each statue is twenty-one meters tall, chiseled directly out of a sandstone cliff face. The idea was to impress the power of Ramses in Egypt upon any stray Nubians who happened to wander in from Sudan in the south. Despite Ramses' efforts, this temple on the west bank of the Nile was eventually forgotten. It was buried by sand like so many other ruins. Ramses' monument inspired British poet Shelley to write his famous work, *Ozymandias*. The poem describes a great ruler conquered by time. The temple remained covered in sand until 1813 when, according to the tour guides, European explorers were led to the site by a local boy. The boy's name was Abu Simbel, and his name means "ear of corn."

After an early morning ride in a minivan, I arrived at Abu Simbel before the crowds or any of the luxury cruise ships. The temple, some 280 kilometres southwest of Aswan, is not in its original location. In the 1960s, the Egyptian government decided to build the Aswan Dam. The hydroelectric dam blocked the flow of the Nile, created Lake Nasser, and drowned the original site of Abu Simbel. When it was announced that the dam was about to be constructed, UNESCO swung into action. UNESCO raised $40 million (US) to cut the temple into blocks and reassemble them on an artificial mountain created at the present location, safely above the water behind the dam. The work was done skillfully. I could not discern where the stone had been cut, nor where reinforcing resin or concrete had been used.

I explored both the main temple and the adjacent smaller one built for Nefertari, the favourite wife of Ramses II. Inside, both temples have impressive statues and carvings on the stone walls. Outside, tourists were free to climb and scramble around the surrounding cliffs. I was one of many tourists taking photographs of Ramses' statues outside, glowering over the calm blue of Lake Nasser under a perfect sky. After feeling the awe, I headed back to the town of Aswan as the heat of the desert was becoming oppressive.

Every ancient country seems to have its own primitive single-sail boat. In Zanzibar, I went on a snorkeling trip on a *dhow*; in Egypt, backpackers tour the Nile on a *felucca*. After the visit to Abu Simbel, it was time to get a group of backpackers together to charter a felucca in Aswan town, and tour the historic ruins along the Nile to the north. It was easy. Or at least all the travel guidebooks tell you it was easy. It was easy to ask at the docks for a felucca captain looking to be chartered. I negotiated a price, per person, for the captain to take a party of seven on the boat for four days. However, it did not feel easy as I spent the next three days trying to cobble together a group of seven passengers. Every backpacker I met was either not interested, had arrived as part of a felucca group already, or opted out of my proposed group at the last minute.

I did manage eventually. I got commitments from a Belgian fellow and a Portuguese youth staying at the YMCA. They proved good companions, particularly the Belgian guy who was a scarred survivor of the Portuguese civil war. Next were Uli and Inge, a couple from West Germany who had arrived and chosen to stay at the same Aswan hotel as me.

Then I found Georgina (Georgie) from London, travelling with her friend Angela from Perth, Australia. Georgie and Angela would be happy to join my group. However, they explained that they needed to break a previous agreement they had made with a shady Egyptian who called himself Rambo. Georgie and Angela were in the same process as me, trying to corral a group of backpackers for Rambo to take on his felucca. But the girls did not feel comfortable with Rambo and had second thoughts about being trapped with him on a boat for several days.

I accompanied the girls down to the Aswan docks to break the news to Captain Rambo. We found him near his vessel, smoking a cigarette. He looked up with a broad grin upon spotting the girls, but his face clouded when they explained they had changed their minds. Rambo was not happy. He started verbally abusing Georgie and Angela and swearing in Arabic.

As Rambo shouted, he stepped closer to the girls to physically intimidate them. I moved to intercede, putting myself between Rambo and my friends. Rambo snarled at me with a maniacal gleam in his eyes. Viciously, he snapped, "You are not my God! You are slitting my throat, and I will do the same to you!" I could feel flecks of spittle flying from his mouth.

I decided the girls were right to trust their instincts and not trap themselves on a boat with this unhinged individual. We backed away from Rambo, watching in case he did pull out a knife.

We made our way towards the restaurant area of the town. Soon, we were in a cozy bar, recovering from the trauma.

Shortly afterwards, I introduced Georgie and Angela to the other members of our completed felucca group. Everyone was now excited with anticipation. We agreed to rendezvous at the dock in two days to depart in the morning, after purchasing supplies of bottled water and snacks.

Finding an honest felucca boat captain was like looking for a shark without teeth. I had negotiated an agreed price per person, for seven persons to take a trip of three nights and four days. On the morning of departure at the waterside, the captain however informed me there would be nine passengers on the boat. The Egyptian surprised us with an East German girl and her Austrian boyfriend.

It was only in October of the previous year that East and West Germany had formally re-unified after four decades of the cold war. The new girl, Heike, had grown up in communist East Germany. She was a ringer for supermodel Paulina Porizkova. Heike was highly amused at the fact that I was ethnically Chinese, a citizen of Canada, and I went by the very German-sounding name of Carl. Growing up in her native East German community, that combination was simply preposterous.

We did not have much of a choice but to accept the increased crowding on the felucca. On the other hand, Uli and Inge seemed happy to welcome more German-speaking passengers.

Unfortunately, conflict between the German bloc and the Anglo group of English-speaking travelers began as soon as the felucca left Aswan. Uli and Inge were miffed that they had not been able to find us Anglos for joint meal planning. We Anglos (including the Belgian and Portuguese guys) were all more individualistic. The notion of planning and eating meals together on the felucca had not even occurred to any of us. Over the next three days, significant cultural differences emerged as the Germans spent all their time as a unit: preparing shared meals and eating together; touring each Egyptian monument as a group of four; and even all going to sleep at the same time. Their conformity was extreme. I still find it hard to believe the days went as smoothly as they did between the Germans and Anglos on that small boat. I think it is best described as mutual ostracizing by the two groups.

One thing that was common between the Anglos and the German bloc was that we were all environmentally-conscious young people. Every backpacker took care to stow their plastic empty after finishing a bottle of water, returning it to the cardboard carton with the remaining full bottles. We were planning to take our cartons of empties off the boat with us after the last day, to dispose of properly on land. We did not guess that I would wake up on the boat early on the last morning of the trip just in time to see the captain calmly chucking the last of the empty plastic bottles into the Nile and flattening the cardboard boxes. It was Mahabalipuram all over again.

Our felucca proceeded north from Aswan on the Nile River, carried by the current. Daytime temperatures were hot, but we either enjoyed a constant cool breeze on the river or had all disembarked to explore ruins on land. Nights on the boat were cool, but not cold. The river was so calm and consistent that the entire boat journey was like riding a giant "lazy river" channel at a pool in a luxury resort hotel. It was fascinating to see the long thin strip of green adorning the riverbanks on both sides, with barren shifting sand dunes starting right behind the vegetated strips. The sand stretched into the distance as far as the eye could see. Village women on the shore did laundry in the pale light of sunrise or sunset. They stared or waved as we passed in the felucca.

Women and girls on the shore of the Nile River, Egypt.

Our first stop was the unusual double temple at Kom Ombo, with one side dedicated to Sobek the crocodile god of strength, and the other dedicated to Horus the falcon-headed god of the sky. Then we visited the Temple of Horus at Edfu. The highlight was our final stop at Luxor, with the Valley of Kings on the opposite side of the river.

No one can fail to be impressed at Luxor. Luxor is what remains of Thebes, the ancient capital of the pharaohs from 2040 to 1750 BCE, and then again from 1550 to 1070 BCE. The modern name of Luxor comes from the Arabic *El-Uqsur*, meaning "the palaces." That term may have referred to the ruins still visible in the desert sands long after the glory of Thebes had faded, with the temples half-buried before the modern Egyptian government discovered its cash cow. The Luxor site includes the Avenue of Sphinxes, Luxor Temple, and the giant Temple of Karnak. There is an obelisk twenty-three meters high, whose twin was transported to Paris as a gift from the Egyptian government. Enormous statues of Ramses

II are everywhere. Just across the Nile from Luxor are the tombs of the pharaohs in the legendary Valley of Kings.

Late in the morning, the captain tied up our boat at the Luxor dock on the east bank, alongside several other feluccas. True to our natures, the German bloc set off as a unit, while the Anglos scattered. The Belgian and Portuguese guys went their separate solitary ways. I explored with Georgie and Angela. All of us felucca passengers walked around Luxor in travel-worn shorts and t-shirts. The vast majority of tourists already wandering the site, however, were fresh-looking, well-dressed Europeans and Americans. They had spewed out from dozens of cruise ships, parked in large berths north of the felucca docks. Everywhere, tourists were greeted by local Muslim women clad in black, calling out, "Hello. Baksheesh!" Since it was so easy to spot a cruise-ship passenger, I wondered why any of these local beggars even bothered to target frugal backpackers.

The clear purpose of Luxor is to rake in international currency. The Egyptian government has widened the streets and demolished local housing to enhance tourist appeal, views, and access. In addition to numerous separate and nested admission fees for the various structures within Luxor, there were ubiquitous papyrus and alabaster "factories."

Ancient Egyptians used papyrus, a weed growing along the banks of the Nile, to make paper. In the Egypt of today, papyrus factories sell sheets of papyrus paper painted with hieroglyphics and scenes inspired by images from inside the temples and tombs.

Alabaster is a soft, fine-grained sedimentary rock that is translucent up to an inch thick. In ancient times, carved and polished alabaster was used to make sculptures and containers, including jars to hold a pharaoh's mummified organs. Today, alabaster factories in Luxor sell alabaster trinkets to tourists.

While Angela decided to stay and spend more time exploring Luxor, Georgie and I took the ferry across the Nile to the west bank. Once there, we hired a taxi to take us to the Temple of Hatshepsut and the Valley of Kings. In a ploy used worldwide to squeeze out more tourist dollars, the taxi driver provided us with a "rest stop" on the two-kilometre drive. He pulled in to his preferred alabaster factory. The driver, by prior arrangement, gets a cut of any sales or a commission for bringing his tourist passengers to the shopkeeper.

With Georgie, I went into the alabaster shop. It was identical to the dozens clamoring for attention on the Luxor side, although the shopkeeper claimed his prices were lower. The shelves and display tables were crammed with overwhelming arrays of useless dust-collectors: false vases, miniature pyramids, miniature Sphinxes, and King Tut heads. I told the shop owner he would make a lot more money selling objects that could be functional as well as decorative. I suggested book ends, vases that could really hold water and cut flowers, or alabaster bowls and mugs. The shopkeeper shrugged, unconvinced. He assured me that tourists demanded the items that he had on display. Georgie and I showed polite interest in the merchandise, but neither of us bought anything. After the obligatory inspection of the shop, we returned to the taxi and continued our day trip.

The Valley of Kings came about when the pharaohs got tired of having their ancestors' tombs plundered and emptied by tomb robbers. It took only a thousand years for the rulers of Egypt to realize that their giant stone pyramids were colossal billboards visible from afar, showing thieves exactly where to find the hoarded riches. The pharaohs began instead to hide their tombs in the Valley of Kings, starting with pharaoh Thutmose I in 1539 BCE. Over the next five hundred years, about sixty-three tombs were constructed. Probably the most famous is the tomb of a minor boy-king, Tutankhamun. His tomb is famous today because it was the only one discovered by modern archeologists that had not been previously emptied by tomb raiders.

In the Valley of Kings, Georgie and I spent hours visiting the once-hidden tombs of famous pharaohs. We explored the burial places for King Tutankhamun, Seti I, Amenhotep II, and several of the Ramses. The tombs were humid with the sweat of tourists. The atmosphere inside them was like neglected basements or underground garages. I hoped that the Egyptian government would soon take steps to preserve the painted hieroglyphics which were peeling and deteriorating on the interior walls.

We spent long hot hours walking in the baking sun. Anyone who has visited these ruins will remember the dry rocky serpentine valley paths going past numerous jumbled rockfalls covering the cliff faces. I think that artificially triggered rockfalls, indistinguishable from those occurring naturally, were used to hide the entrances of the tombs after they were sealed. Several touts followed us, hoping we would succumb and pay for a donkey ride, like their camel-jockey counterparts at Giza.

Late in the day, Georgie and I returned by taxi to Luxor for dinner and to spend the night. Crowds of tourists were leaving the temples, coalescing into groups as each cruise ship sounded its horn to signal that it was time to depart. Lines of cruise passengers formed behind the gangplank for their assigned boat. Everyone was smiling. Clutched by almost every person in line was a recently purchased roll of papyrus, as well as an alabaster vase, miniature pyramid, miniature Sphinx, or King Tut head.

28. WAITING IN DAHAB

AFTER LUXOR, IT was time to experience a different side of Egypt. I made my way back to Cairo, then left immediately for the Sinai Peninsula. I was headed to the beach for a few days of relaxation.

It was a nine-hour bus ride. The bus crossed the Suez Canal, proceeded southwest along the coast of the peninsula with a gorgeous view of the sea from the highway, rounded the southernmost point, and went through the luxury resort town of Sharm El-Sheikh. The waters of the Red Sea near Sharm were proclaimed as the best scuba-diving site on earth by Jacques Cousteau himself, the man who invented scuba (Self-Contained Underwater Breathing Apparatus). Sharm was where you could spend two hundred US dollars a day for a hotel room and food, plus extra for scuba-diving excursions. That price sounds reasonable to me today, but it was a princely sum for a backpacker in 1991. I took a pass. Instead, I continued on the bus to Dahab, another vagabond retreat in the spirit of Kathmandu, or Khaosan Road in Bangkok. Rooms in Dahab were two Egyptian pounds per night (about sixty cents Canadian), or you could simply sleep on the beach.

The sleepy backpacker retreat of Dahab was bordered by a Bedouin village to the south, and lay on the Gulf of Aqaba, the eastern ear of the Red Sea. Dahab was a place of date palm oases, camels, young Israeli sun worshippers, humid nights, flies, and absolutely incredible snorkeling. It is said that after diving in the vivid aquascape of the Red Sea, all other scuba-diving sites will seem pale and washed out in comparison. Whether it is my memory or imagination, I must agree. Except for the unspoiled reefs near the Hog Islands in Honduras, I've not had another diving or snorkeling experience since that comes close to that magical underwater beauty at Dahab.

Stepping off the bus, I canvassed the town and found a modest establishment with simple beach huts for rent. Shortly after settling in, I learned that Dahab had some uniquely Egyptian quirks.

In Dahab, the standard operating procedure at the restaurants was to wait almost precisely one hour to be served. No kidding; we timed it with our watches. It did not matter what you ordered or at which restaurant. Whether you asked for a fruit salad, pizza, grilled fish, or just a bottled soft drink, you waited an hour for your food or beverage to be brought to your table. We experimented with different restaurants and ordering different menu items to see if faster service would result. It was to no avail. The Dahab restaurants had reached some sort of pact for this prescribed waiting time along the entire beach community. In addition, all the restaurants had agreed to play music from only two compact disk albums: Phil Collins' *But Seriously*, and Sinead O'Conner's *Nothing Compares 2 U*. These were played exclusively, over and over.

Another quirk was that Dahab was "dry." It was not that alcohol was prohibited. Beer was readily available in Egypt, even though the country is Muslim. The labels on locally-brewed bottles of beer clearly stated an alcohol content of 2.5 percent, plus or minus 2 percent. Rather, alcoholic drinks in Dahab were only available at the single restaurant in town that possessed a liquor license. Further, that restaurant had no supply of beer, wine, or spirits on the day I arrived. The owner of the eatery had not paid enough *baksheesh* to local police. In response, the police put a blockade on alcoholic shipments to the restaurant. This, I was informed, was a regular occurrence.

Dahab had a truly international crowd. I hung out with backpackers Martin from Holland, Bernat from Spain, and Kurt from Washington State, USA. I liked self-deprecating Martin the most. Martin sported short, sandy blond hair, clear blue eyes, a square jaw, and a trim build. Martin joked that he needed to travel to feel physically "normal," because he was so short compared to the Dutch population at home. He was my height, 5'8", but I wasn't offended.

Martin, Bernat, Kurt and I embarked on long political discussions and traded travel anecdotes every night. We sipped soft drinks and periodically asked when the beer would arrive. One evening the restaurant staff finally assured us that beer would come the next day.

The following morning was just as warm and inviting as every morning before. After breakfast with Martin, I rented a snorkel mask and fins. I set out free-diving from the shore in front of the beach bungalow cluster. Free-diving is simply holding your breath and swimming down to hang out with the undersea life for as long as you can before surfacing for air. I was actually quite good at free-diving, able to descend repeatedly for up to a minute and a half. Apparently, with some training, many physically fit people can free-dive for up to four minutes on a single breath.

The shallow tides, high salinity, and consistently warm sun on the Gulf of Aqaba have led to unusually vivid colors in the coral reefs. They are full of soft corals waving in the gentle current, including whip corals and gorgeous gorgonian fans up to two meters wide. Butterfly fish, starfish, and parrotfish were abundant, as well as anemones with resident clownfish. Clownfish were popularized as the main characters in the animated film *Finding Nemo* (2003).

I swam south, systematically exploring parallel to the beach. The most vivid colors are in the shallow water where corals benefit from abundant sunlight. I wore a t-shirt to prevent sunburn, and it was impossible to get cold in that crystal-clear water. I swam along the level shelf of the reef. Looking down where the reef dropped off on the seaward crest made me feel dizzy with vertigo, as the water quickly became dark in the mysterious depths. It was weird, because I felt like I could "fall" into the depths, even though I was floating in water.

Many corals were red and purple. I wondered if they had inspired the name for the Red Sea. I discovered giant clams and tiny seahorses, and even a couple of rarely seen lionfish. At one point, I thought I saw a turtle swimming away in the distance. I lost track of time, continuing in the direction of the Bedouin village for at least an hour. Finally, fatigued and with a slight headache, I left the water at the southern end of Dahab town. I removed the constricting, stretchy band of the snorkel mask and kicked off my fins. I walked along the shore back towards my beach hut, feeling very satisfied.

What I did not realize was that Martin had caught a glimpse of me just as I had gone under the waves at the start of the day. And then he didn't see me again. After twenty minutes, Martin was concerned. And after half an hour, he began combing the beach, asking everyone he met if they had seen "a Chinese boy" in the water.

Poor Martin! His relief was evident as I approached him halfway back to the bungalow. I bought him several beers that night. But we did have to wait an hour after ordering for the beer to arrive at our table.

29. LAST DAYS IN CAIRO

"*REGARDE! IL Y A des gens la bas!*"

According to Jews, Christians, and Muslims, Mount Sinai on the Sinai Peninsula of Egypt is the place where Moses was given the biblical Ten Commandments by God. The French tour group trudged up Mount Sinai in the middle of the night. Towards dawn, they navigated the final bends on the winding camel path. The route was well-worn but littered with loose stones making it easy to trip in the darkness. The tourists had walked for about three hours with gradual elevation gain, reaching the only steep section in the last few meters before the summit. There, they were astonished when their flashlights illuminated backpackers just waking on sleeping mats, already at the top.

I yawned and sat up with a flashlight shining in my eyes. The French tourists were shadows about thirty feet away. Several more organized tour groups crowded up behind them. I could hear voices in Italian too. It was chilly, but my sleeping bag had been warm enough under the spectacular starry night. The weather gods were kind; there had been no clouds and only a mild breeze. As an added bonus, it was my first restful night in many because the mosquitoes had been vanquished by the night wind. I stretched, and along with my backpacker companions, rolled up my sleeping bag and got ready to photograph the sunrise.

Unlike the organized tourist groups, our party of backpackers had walked the incredible landscape at leisure in the warmth of day with the mountain virtually to ourselves. We had trekked up past steep rocky ravines and barren hills. For someone from urban Toronto, Canada, the mauve and rust coloured rock formations of the desert landscape were mysteriously beautiful and otherworldly. Food and snacks were available from refreshment stands near St. Catherine's Monastery at the base. More refreshments were available from kiosks on a rocky terrace a few meters away from the summit. Since we saw hardly a blade of grass in the sea of rock during the ascent, I thought finding any bush at the peak would be a miracle, much less the burning bush that had greeted Moses.

View from the camel path to the summit of Mount Sinai.
Note the backpackers in the foreground on the left.

We had settled in at the top as the sun was weakening. Shadows grew long as the reddening disk went down behind row upon row of jagged sandstone ridges. The Arab vendors closed up their refreshment stands and disappeared somewhere for the night. The desert went silent in pinks and purples. Including my group of seven, a total of maybe twenty backpackers enjoyed the serenity of the summit.

With nightfall, slow satellites and fast meteorites put on a show as they crossed the vast black backdrop of stationary stars.

There is scholarly debate on whether Mount Sinai is, in fact, the spot where God revealed himself to Moses. However, a shrine to the burning bush was first built on Mount Sinai in 337 CE by Helena, the mother of Roman Emperor Constantine. At 2,285 m, Mount Sinai is the second highest peak on the peninsula. The actual climb from the desert below was only about 685 meters. The summit is famous as a place to watch the sunrise.

With the arrival of hundreds in organized tours about half an hour before dawn, we backpackers had already staked out prime real estate for the view. Still rubbing the sleep from my eyes, the summit became crowded and noisy. Then everyone went silent in the minutes before sunrise. Next, the *click click* of cameras filled the air as everyone captured the sun climbing up over the layers of rocky ridges stretching into the horizon. I enjoyed the visual beauty of the sunrise. However, I think that for a lot of people on that summit, it was a religious pilgrimage.

Backpackers on the summit of Mount Sinai.
The author is the guy with wild black hair at the back, center.

After the sun illuminated the desert, it seemed only a few minutes before we backpackers had the summit to ourselves again. The organized tour groups departed as quickly as they had come. They were hurrying down to catch their buses awaiting below. I bought a light breakfast from the concession stands and munched contentedly as the air warmed up with day. Then, still travelling with my backpacker group, I took the steeper and more direct route down from the summit, the 3,750 Steps of Penitence.

The Steps of Penitence, or Repentance, lead back down to St. Catherine's Monastery. According to legend, most of these rough stone steps were carved by a single monk in the sixth century CE. He built the steps as a self-imposed punishment for an unknown sin he had committed. Others finished his work when this monk died, just before he was able to complete the last few steps to the top. Bummer.

In Cairo again, I spent my time exploring and enjoying the atmosphere of the old city. I was economizing, anticipating the expense of Europe on the next stage of my journey. Meals were mostly from food carts on the street: *fuul* (fava beans mashed up with onions and spices) in a pita bread pocket and pickled vegetables; or *shawarma*, slices of roast lamb in a pita bread roll. For variety, I tried pigeon. I wondered if they came from pigeon farms or were just caught in local city parks. There is not much meat on a pigeon, I discovered. I stopped ordering them after I was still hungry after pigeon dinners on two occasions. Once, from a street vendor, I purchased a mound of spaghetti noodles with fried onions and hot sauce for lunch. It was the first time I'd eaten something that I felt burn my mouth, burn down my throat, burn in my gut, and continue burning my anus on its way out a few hours later.

The narrow streets of old Cairo were a congested maze. I walked through the bazaar district, Khan el-Khalili. The bazaar had great charm, despite having become a tourist trap. It was still full of small, open-front single-room family businesses. There was a father and son team building chandeliers, another shop where craftsmen built wooden chairs, and still another where family members strapped pre-cut wood slats together with metal bands and hand tools to assemble water-tight pails and barrels. Each factory shop displayed its completed products nested and neatly stacked for sale. As I sauntered past, these Egyptian shopkeepers and craftsmen smiled at me the instant they spotted my camera.

In the Cairo camel market, black men from Nubia with skin as dark as ink haggled with lighter-skinned Arabs. The Nubians had brought the camels from southern Sudan by a thirteen-day trek. The camel market was busy, despite the ongoing Second Sudanese Civil War. That war had prevented me from travelling to Egypt overland from Kenya through Sudan. The war had started 1983, and would not end until 2005, becoming the second longest civil war in history.

Camels can survive drought conditions even after herds of cattle, sheep, and goats have died off. Camels are beasts of burden, used for racing in Saudi Arabia, and to provide milk for the Turkana nomads in the desert. However, in Egypt camels are bought mostly to either carry tourists, or to slaughter for meat. Curiously, I don't remember seeing camel on an Egyptian menu.

Islamic Cairo was a city filled by men and boys; the streets were devoid of women except for female tourists. Everywhere, middle-aged men with calloused and dirty bare feet were smoking *shisha* from ornate Arabian water pipes, called *hookahs*. Shisha and coffee houses, or *"ahwas,"* were ubiquitous. Since the Middle Ages, Egyptian men have sprawled in ahwas to complain about their lives or wives or politics.

Shisha smoking might look exotic, but the smoke is from ordinary tobacco. Shisha is made by mixing dried tobacco leaves with molasses or honey, adding fruit (mostly apple) for flavour, and compressing the mash into clumps. The clumps are put into a compartment at the top of the hookah pipe and burning hot coals are placed on the shisha to generate smoke. You suck on the mouthpiece to draw the smoke from the top chamber down through a tube into the water in the hookah. The smoke then bubbles up and is sucked through the hose into your mouth. The water cools the smoke and makes it "smooth." However, the water-cooled smoke contains the same amount of nicotine, tar, and other noxious substances found in cigarette smoke; it is addictive and carcinogenic. Regular cigarette smokers say that nicotine, the addictive drug in tobacco, produces a feeling that is simultaneously alert and calm. I don't know the statistics of lung cancer amongst habitual shisha smokers.

Egyptian men enjoying *shisha* at a coffee house in Cairo.

I spent a leisurely afternoon with an American friend, Dan, at an ahwas in the bazaar. The server at the hookah café gave us pipes that were lit and ready to enjoy. I had never bought a pack of cigarettes in my life. In my twenties, I was an infrequent smoker, puffing on perhaps a dozen cigarettes a year from friends at nightclubs during graduate school. Every New Year's Eve, I ceremoniously smoked a single cigar with a glass of cognac. Traditionally, hookah smoke is not inhaled, but simply held in the mouth and enjoyed like cigar smoke before exhaling. I didn't know this at the time. I took the hookah smoke right into my lungs. It felt similar to cigarette smoke but had a hint of fruity taste.

Dan was one of the few backpackers I met who was older than me, in his early thirties. He had been in Egypt for over three months. He had short, straight black hair, horn-rimmed glasses, and looked a bit malnourished from an insufficient diet in Cairo. Dan was also pale, somehow staying untanned from the Egyptian sun. Unlike Thierry or other backpackers, Dan seemed to have little interest in touring Egypt's historic monuments. Instead, Dan was content to spend day after day going for walks in Cairo bazaars and smoking shisha. He was unhurried, never agitated, and explained that once a tout had pestered him for the third time, he would just tell the tout to piss off (actually using more colorful language), and they never bothered him again. Dan admitted that he was not sure when he would be ready to go back to the United States.

Dan breathed in a long draw from his hookah. "All ex-patriots," he informed me, "are maladjusted to their own society."

Muslims have obligatory prayers at five times each day. As Dan and I were enjoying our hookah pipes, the call started for *Asr*, the afternoon prayer. The muezzin's singsong voice came from a nearby loudspeaker mounted high on a utility pole: "*Allahu Akbar* (God is Great) ..."

It was Dan's considered opinion that the next threat to world peace was Islam. It scared him. From his travels in the Arabian Peninsula, Dan was convinced Islam demanded intolerance of other faiths. Dan believed that for many of Islam's Arabic followers, religious intolerance had grown into hatred.

I was skeptical of Dan's concerns. None of the Arab states were nuclear powers. It was long before the technology of fracking transformed many more countries into oil and gas-exporting nations. In 1991, Saudi Arabia and the Arab (and Muslim) states of OPEC, the Organization of Petroleum Exporting Countries, were raking in the cash. Perhaps Saudi Arabia and OPEC could choke off the world's supply of oil and gasoline, but hardly engage in a world war. How could these nations of Islam possibly threaten the world?

Dan had no answer, but he was convinced that Islam would find a way to make all non-believers feel unsafe.

Ten years later in 2001, the Islamic terrorist group al-Quaida destroyed New York's World Trade Center by flying hijacked passenger planes into the centre's two skyscrapers. Al-Quaida killed 3,000 civilians in those towers. By 2019, Islamic terrorists had killed scores of people in London, Manchester, Paris, Madrid, St. Petersburg, Barcelona, Stockholm, Berlin, and other European cities through seemingly random attacks over the years. A few "radicalized" Muslim individuals carried out attacks in the United States. Attackers used bombs, suicide-bombers, trucks driving through crowds, semi-automatic rifles, guns, or even knives. In these attacks, the killers invariably shouted out loud "*Allahu Akbar!*"

Of course, except for the World Trade Center attack, the annual number of people killed by Muslim terrorists is tiny compared to the number who die each month in mass shootings in the US, killed by their fellow Americans. Total deaths by terrorism is nothing compared to the average of 11,000 shooting deaths in the

US every year. That number excludes suicides. Shockingly, only about 500 of these annual gun deaths, or less than 5 percent, are from the so-called "mass shootings" covered so heavily by the US news media.

On one of my last days in Egypt, I visited the great Mosque of Mohammed Ali atop the Citadel. The mosque is seen by many as a symbol of the country. The mosque was built between 1830 and 1848 by Muhammad Ali Pasha, the founder of modern Egypt.

That morning, like every other, began with the sound of Muslim prayers. The prayers blared out from megaphones attached to poles or high points on mosques throughout the city. Although all three of the great pyramids of Giza were originally covered in polished limestone, the limestone had been carried away for other building projects over the ages, especially to build mosques as the nation of Egypt turned to Islam.

In the religion of Islam, there is only one god whose name is Allah, and his messenger, or prophet, was a man named Muhammad. Islam originated with Muhammad, who was born in the year 570 CE in the city of Mecca, Saudi Arabia. In the year 610, Muhammad reported that he had been visited by the angel Gabriel, while Muhammad was praying in a cave near Mecca. This was the same angel Gabriel of Judaism and Christianity. Gabriel told Muhammad that there is only one god, Allah, and that Jesus, Adam, Abraham, Noah, Moses, and Muhammad himself were all prophets of Allah.

Muhammed said that there will be a Day of Judgment when Allah decides whether each and every human being will go to heaven or hell, and that Allah demands obedience. *Islam* is actually the Arabic word for "submission." Muhammad preached that Allah's teachings had been misinterpreted or were flawed in the religions of the Jews and the Christians. Rather than preaching a message of love, Muhammad became a public speaker asking everyone to "submit" to Allah's will.

Unsurprisingly, Muhammad was not very popular when he started asking everyone to submit. Muhammad moved from Mecca to Medina to escape his ensuing persecution. Over the years, however, Muhammad was somehow able to persuade more and more people to adopt his new religion. First Medina, then Mecca, and then every city in western Arabia converted to Islam. Some say that Muhammad's armies forced defeated Arab tribes to convert to Islam or die. Others claim that Muhammad's battles were all in self-defence against attackers; that the Quran itself says that forcing the conquered to accept Islam is hypocritical; and that Muhammad gained converts only by preaching and persuasion.

Believers of Islam call themselves Muslims. Muslims try to follow rules set out in the Quran, the Muslim holy book. These rules include the Five Pillars: Declare that you believe there is only one god, his name is Allah, and his prophet is Muhammad; pray five times a day while facing in the direction of the city of Mecca; give to charity in proportion to your personal wealth; abstain from food and beverages during Ramadan, the ninth month of the Islamic lunar calendar; and journey to the city of Mecca at least once in your lifetime. This journey, or pilgrimage, is called the *hajj*, and involves more rituals such as touching or kissing the *Kaaba*, or Black Stone, in Mecca. The Quran also sets out Islamic law, the Shariah law so popular in Pakistan.

After Muhammad died in 632 CE, he was succeeded by Caliph Abu Bakr. This Caliph sent his generals forth from Mecca, Saudi Arabia. In the year 641, Muslim armies led by Amr ibn al-Aas proceeded west across the Sinai Peninsula and added Egypt to the Nation of Islam. Islam then spread across the entire Middle East.

Today, Islam is one of the largest religions in the world with almost two billion believers. I mused about what sort of things could provide objective evidence that an angel had communicated with Muhammad. Of course, that was silly. I realized that thinking and logic would not lead me to embrace any of the religions I had encountered on my travels. Every devout person I met either told me they simply believed their religion or did not understand my questions about proof. On the train to Karachi in Pakistan, an older Muslim man appeared baffled by my queries. Knitting his eyebrows, the man said, "What do you mean? The Quran itself is proof that the Quran is the work of God."

30. REAL MEN IN MADRID

FROM CAIRO, I FLEW by KLM airlines to Amsterdam. The shock of European prices hit hard. It was impossible to survive a day without spending at least twenty Canadian dollars. That was back in 1991. But even though I had to skip one or two dinners to save money, it was still a huge relief to be free of mosquitoes and enjoy European bathrooms and beer. Amsterdam brought the first touch of rain on my skin since the lightning storm in Serengeti Park three months ago. I resumed my dance with the clouds. After visiting Anne Frank House and taking some leisurely walks along the Amstel River in the rain, I boarded a train to drier weather in Paris.

I had visited Paris twice before, and so I spent my days there re-acquainting with favourite sites. I went to the Eiffel tower, the Musee Rodin, and Notre Dame Cathedral. But my thoughts were mostly on re-uniting with Mariana in Madrid at last. It was not long before I was on another train.

Although it was September, it seemed autumn had not yet arrived at the city of Madrid; it was pleasantly warm and dry. Daytime temperatures still reached the high twenties, and I was comfortable in shorts and a t-shirt. I made my way from the train station to the city's subway and proceeded to the stop nearest to where Mariana lived. When we finally met up outside her apartment, I had the overwhelming feeling of coming home. Mariana was just as I remembered, and we embraced spontaneously in the street.

I fell in love again with Mariana, and soon became enamored with the Spanish lifestyle too. However, over the next few weeks, the daunting reality of shaping a new life for myself in this foreign land also hit me. I discovered that my travelers' Spanish, quite adequate for backpacking, was hopelessly inadequate for daily life in Madrid. I could ask for a hotel room with air-conditioning. I could ask for red wine or beer. But I could not explain in Spanish that I needed a hex key to adjust a cable on my rented bicycle, because I couldn't shift all the way down to first gear.

It would be a steep learning curve before I could even start to put any effort into earning a living. And how would I do that? Taking any old job to pay the bills would be far more difficult in a foreign language. I had no skills as a baker. Nor could I wait on tables in Spanish. I didn't have a clue about making contacts at the local university, either, to inquire about work in the research labs there.

Of course, it was not impossible for a foreigner to adapt to life in Spain. Mariana introduced me to her friend Debbie, an American who had lived in Madrid for thirteen years. Debbie had been passionate about all things Spain since she was a teenager. She improved on her high-school Spanish in the United States. When she was comfortably fluent, she built relationships and took steps to live and work in Spain as a writer and translator.

Mariana, Debbie, me, and another friend, Claudia, spent a weekend exploring the historic Castile region near Madrid on bicycles. Every small town had a central plaza, fountain, and church. We pedalled through hot dry weather with only the rare lonely cumulus cloud. Along the way, Debbie provided a continuous stream of geographical and historical trivia. The seemingly endless tales of bravery, star-crossed lovers' suicides, haunted abandoned castle ruins, folk legends, and anecdotes in Debbie's head made it clear that she was in Spain because she loved every inch of it. Perhaps because of Debbie, I began to wonder if I had what it takes to stay in the country.

After the bicycle trip, the weeks with Mariana seemed like one long *tapas* festival. *Tapas* are small savory appetizers served with drinks at a bar. Common tapas dishes include slices of cheese, mixed olives, chorizo sausage, fresh marinated prawns, and fried squid. The literal meaning of tapa is "lid." It is believed that tapas began when people in southern Spain used a small saucer of cheese or ham as a lid for a glass of wine to keep out flies. Spaniards use the verb *"tapear"* to mean going from bar to bar with friends for drinks and tapas. And that is exactly what we did every night.

To celebrate Mariana's birthday, we went to a South American dance bar. The ability of this small and slender girl to hold her liquor was nothing short of miraculous. In between dancing, the two of us downed a pitcher of sangria, a bottle of rose wine, followed by several pints of beer, finishing the evening with rum and coke. She matched me ounce for ounce in alcohol. Mariana then drove us home; I was hammered. The next morning at 8:30 a.m., Mariana was up, perky as ever, and left for work while I nursed a hangover. Still, I pulled myself together to go out for more tapas that evening.

Tourists may get the impression that this tapas lifestyle was cheap for local Spaniards. According to Mariana, it was not. It was simply that the priorities of the Spanish lifestyle dictated that a large portion of disposable income be spent on tapas nights, meaning almost every night of the week. The Spanish just love getting together and talking about their lives while grazing on tasty appetizers and de-stressing from the day with alcohol.

Just as she was on Fiji, Mariana continued to be a whirlwind of energy. Now she took me to one party after another. I became convinced that Spain has the world's most beautiful women and the planet's ugliest ties. But eventually, the good times came to an end.

Mariana and I spent our last evening together at Las Cuevas de Luis Candelas restaurant in Madrid. In the 1800s, Candelas was a bandit who used the caves at the back of the restaurant as a hideout. In 1949, bullfighter Felix Diez bought the caves, and turned them into the restaurant that still operates today. Las Cuevas is one of the oldest continually operating restaurants in the world.

At Las Cuevas, I mentioned that I would have liked to have seen the traditional Running of the Bulls in Pamplona. Unfortunately, that event had occurred earlier in July before I arrived Spain. This is an event where a group of bull cattle, usually six, are goaded to stampede along a fenced-in path through the city streets. The bulls are of a breed of cattle that have horns. Men show off their bravery by jumping into the path ahead of the charging animals along their route. The men run in front of the bulls, and leap over the barricades on either side at the last minute to avoid being gored or trampled by the raging beasts.

The Running of the Bulls is believed to have started when bulls were transported from the outskirts of Pamplona to the bullfighting ring in the town centre. To speed up the process, the bulls were frightened or prodded to run to their pens at the arena. Young men started to show off by racing in front of the bulls, reaching the safety of the pens ahead of the animals. The Pamplona festival is now held annually in honor of Saint Fermin. The festival lasts nine days, with bulls running in the morning and being killed in bullfights the corresponding afternoon, for each of the nine days.

Mariana took a sip of wine and tossed some spicy *calamares* into her mouth. Sitting in Las Cuevas restaurant, Mariana continued her education of me in all things Spain. She explained that Pamplona is only the most famous of these bull-running events. Many small towns in the region have designated a fiesta day with a local running of the bulls. Mariana expressed disgust that grown men, or overgrown men with beer guts, would engage in this spectacle. She thought it was a cruel taunting of the bulls, and not like "real" bull fighting where a matador would need courage to face down a maddened animal and skill to dodge its horns.

"It's not like a real bullfight," Mariana reiterated. "But it shows the real Spanish men."

"You mean," I asked, "it shows how committed they are to keeping Spanish traditions alive?"

"No," she answered, smirking. "Spanish men are noisy. They tell everyone how brave they are, standing around waiting for the bulls. But when the danger comes, Spanish men run away!"

31. A HISTORY UNPLANNED

I went to the doctor, I went to the mountains
I looked to the children, I drank from the fountains
There's more than one answer to these questions
Pointing me in a crooked line
And the less I seek my source for some definitive
The closer I am to fine
The closer I am to fine, yeah

"Closer to Fine" words and music by Amy Elizabeth Ray
and Emily Ann Saliers (Indigo Girls)

AFTER STAYING WITH Mariana for three weeks, it became obvious that I had no future in a relationship with her or in Spain. Most people usually behave differently while they are travelling than when at home, and Mariana and I were two such people. Or at least Mariana was, since technically I was still traveling. Despite dreaming of being with this girl for months, a few short weeks of reality unmasked the fantasy. We could not spend all our time being together, carefree, exploring at leisure. Reality meant buying groceries and supplies, employment commitments, relationships with other friends and family, cleaning up the home as we lived in it, and managing our emotions when we needed to make joint decisions. A big part of dating is discovering how compatible you are as a couple during difficult, stressful, or unlucky events.

I found less emotional and practical support from Mariana than I had expected for adapting to a life in Spain. She quickly tired of my dependency on her for that support. We had shared some great adventures, but it was time to say our goodbyes.

Over the next month, I threw myself back into adventure-travel mode, trying not to think about my failure with Mariana. I made my way south to visit Seville. I loved the flamenco guitar and flamenco dancing, but I felt sickened watching the bullfights. I then crossed the English Channel to Wales, walked up Mount Snowdon in the rain, and rambled around inside Caernarfon Castle. Eventually I arrived at the city of London.

London, capital of the British Empire, and now after de-colonization, the spiritual centre of the Commonwealth of Nations. The metropolis of London was bursting with history, British culture, and modern money. I shopped in Harrods, the world-famous luxury department store downtown established in 1849. I looked for souvenirs, but it was difficult to find anything that had actually been made in the United Kingdom. Even in 1991, everything in Harrods had been manufactured in China or other countries of the European Economic Community.

Today, Harrods itself is owned by the Arab nation of Qatar. Globalization is a fact of life.

Eventually, I discovered a set of miniature British officer figurines sold as Christmas tree ornaments. The set included London bobbies and kilted Scottish guards. It was the beginning of my lifelong habit of acquiring a small object to use as a Christmas tree ornament from every country I visit. I was shopping in part to get my mind off my relationship woes. Not for the last time, I thought wistfully of Mariana. And so, I did what any other young man would do after failing miserably at a relationship with a girl: I called up another one.

London was home to Georgie, whom I'd last seen at the Egyptian ruins in Luxor. I telephoned Georgie and was happy to hear her chipper and excited British accent. Georgie had long dirty-blonde hair that fell below her shoulders, grey-green eyes, and a cute, narrow pointed nose. She had crow's feet wrinkles at the corners of her eyes from smiling all the time, and she was super skinny.

For the next few evenings, Georgie joined me after she finished her workday as temporary office help. We enjoyed generous meals of fish and chips, or ate cheap burgers from Wimpy's, the English fast-food chain. We saved our cash for pints of beer at traditional British pubs. Georgie introduced me to a different pub every night. When the weekend came, Georgie was able to get away for a couple of days to visit Stonehenge with me. We took a train from London to Salisbury Station, about a half hour away.

Salisbury City is a bus ride away from Stonehenge. Salisbury also boasts a magnificent cathedral built between 1220 and 1258. The main attraction at Salisbury Cathedral is that it houses one of the surviving original copies of the *Magna Carta*. Georgie and I headed to the church to see the famous manuscript.

The *Magna Carta* began as an agreement signed by King John of England in the year 1215. The king was trying to prevent a civil war between himself and the powerful barons of his own country. King John agreed to paragraphs in the *Magna Carta* that guarantee everyone the right to a fair trial, meaning that King John could not simply throw his enemies into prison. Other paragraphs establish, for the first time in history, that the king himself must obey the laws of the land just like everyone else. Of course, King John hated this agreement and cancelled it a year later. Fortunately for the world, King John was killed in the civil war that followed. In an unforeseen turn of events, the *Magna Carta* was revived to ensure peace in the kingdom when nine-year-old Henry III assumed the throne after the civil war was done. Monarchs and governments have been guided by the *Magna Carta* ever since.

For some reason, I had been expecting to see a book or booklet of a few pages. Instead, the *Magna Carta* was a single centuries-old sheepskin page. It was crammed with small, fancy, hand-written letters in Latin, completely illegible to me. Its authors could have had no clue that the document would have such a profound impact on the development of democracy around the world. Many different countries have now copied into their own constitutions those paragraphs guaranteeing the right to a fair trial and ensuring that even the leaders of the land must obey the laws of the land.

After paying homage to the *Magna Carta*, I left with Georgie and we spent the night at a modest hotel. The following morning, we caught the Stonehenge tour bus from the town centre. The ride from Salisbury to the historic site took twenty minutes, passing nondescript rural farms and grassy fields.

The mysterious circle at Stonehenge is often described as being over 5,000 years old. The first structure created by unknown builders around 3,000 BCE, however, was a circular ditch, or *henge*, without any of the giant stones. Just inside the Stonehenge ditch, archaeologists discovered the remains of sixty-four cremations from this time period. Some five hundred years later, at about the same time the Great Pyramids were being built by the pharoahs at Giza, roughly a hundred massive stones were hauled to the Stonehenge ditch and set up in concentric rings. While the inner ring of larger sandstone slabs came from local sources, the outer ring 'bluestones' were quarried in Wales about 200 miles away. No one knows why the Welsh stones were moved to Stonehenge or how. Around 2,000 BCE, the stones at Stonehenge were reorganized into their present iconic arrangement: pairs of upright pillars connected with a horizontal lintel slab above.

The purpose of Stonehenge is even more of a mystery than its construction. Perhaps different peoples built and altered the arrangement of the stones over the millennia for different purposes. Archeologists have determined that Stonehenge was used as a burial site, an astronomical calendar, and a place for ceremonies to mark religious or agricultural events.

Other than stands of trees on the horizon, the standing stones were the only vertical structures to be seen in the flat field of grass. By the time of my visit, it was no longer possible to get within arms' reach of the monument. A paved path led from the parking lot and ran past the northwest edge of the circle. The closest you could get was about thirty feet from the nearest stone along this path. I took a photo from here, thinking at the time that every tourist photographed the same close-up view of Stonehenge from this vantage point. Elsewhere, a rope cordons off a huge circle hundreds of feet away from the monument in the centre. Watchful officials kept tourists from stepping over the rope boundary.

There was a sign posted that proclaimed 700,000 people visited Stonehenge annually. That was almost 2,000 people a day in 1991. The number of daily visitors is no doubt higher today, thirty years later. Perhaps it was because of the weather, but Stonehenge seemed dreary and sad to Georgie and me. The tour bus crowds appeared subdued as well, although everyone was taking photographs. It was as though they were visiting a cemetery, rather than a place to celebrate the solstices or an historic engineering marvel. I guess this was appropriate, given that Stonehenge started as a Stone Age burial site.

Georgie and I savored the mysterious atmosphere surrounding the ancient stone circle. We then took the bus and train back to London. Georgie was a lot of fun. She promised to come and visit me in Canada one day. We said our goodbyes that evening.

In all, I had been living out of a backpack for ten months, or eleven if you included my time in Calgary after leaving my dad's place in Toronto. I decided to spend my last day before returning to Canada in the British Museum in London. On an overcast morning at the end of October, I took a train in the London Underground public transit system (the "Chube") to Tottenham Court Road station and walked to the British Museum.

Originally called the British Museum of Natural History, the building showcased over two hundred years of world-wide collecting (some would say pilfering) by explorers of the British Empire. At its peak in the 1920s, Britain had established the largest empire in human history, controlling a quarter of the world's population and almost a quarter of its land mass area. Britannia truly ruled the waves.

The British Museum started as the private collection of a wealthy doctor, Sir Hans Sloane. The doctor died leaving a will that required his collection to be made available to the public. The requirement was unprecedented. As a result, the world's first public museum opened in 1758. The trustees running the museum were leery of Sir Sloane's radical concept of public access; they knew the lower classes and servants would be up to no good. The first visitors were not allowed to see the exhibits unless accompanied by a museum employee.

Since it first opened in 1758, entrance to the British Museum has been free. I spent hours in its exhibition halls, seeing only a fraction of the museum's collection. Famous items I lingered at included the Egyptian Rosetta Stone, the Greek Parthenon sculptures, and the Anglo-Saxon treasure found at Sutton Hoo. Some exhibits let me relive past travel experiences. Others, like the Aztec rooms, inspired me to visit exotic and fascinating places many years later.

For as long as I could remember, I had struggled. I felt incomplete, and that I would remain inferior or unfinished until I achieved something truly positive and significant. Without becoming at the least a footnote in history, I felt that my life would amount to no more than a wasted opportunity. This was not a case of needing to flatter my ego. I felt vaguely unworthy. I thought I always would, until I could reasonably claim that I had contributed to the collective effort to make the world a better place. That I, too, had pulled my weight. Or else, I would have squandered the investment and sacrifices others had made so that I could enjoy a decent life.

I was always trying so hard to "make my mark." It wasn't because of anything my father had said. He never told me that hard work would be rewarded. He never told me I could achieve whatever I put my mind to. On the contrary, Chan occasionally lamented my bad luck at not being born into a wealthy, well-connected family. No, my need to achieve something—anything—remarkable in life came from within. And most of the time, when I thought about it, I felt this general dissatisfaction at having done nothing notable to speak of so far.

However, leaving the British Museum almost a year after setting out from home, I became aware that I had a new lightness of heart. I smiled. The sunshine did not burst through the clouds on that grey autumn afternoon, but I was serene and at peace. That museum was a showcase of individuals who had, over the course of history, changed the world. You might have thought that seeing the incredible art, technological leaps, and tributes to great leaders would inspire me to try even harder to make my own mark. Far from it.

After months of travel, I had come to accept that each of us human individuals will spend most of a lifetime doing absolutely nothing memorable at all. And that is okay. World-changing events don't happen by intention; they are unforeseen and only understood as world-changing after the fact. The world is just too damn complex and unpredictable. People at the centre of historic world-changing events come into these critical situations through a combination of circumstance, accidents of birth, and forces beyond anyone's control. And why was I being so hard on myself? It was not as though I could earn my way to becoming

Prince Charles. I could not think my way into being as brilliant as Stephen Hawking. I could never acquire the talent of a Lady Gaga by sheer force of will. I could not just talk myself into feeling Craig Kielberger's passion to end child labor.

Around the globe, I had watched people spending their lives in countless forgettable hours. I saw people unloading bags of shrimp feed, sorting tea leaves, herding goats, chewing *khat* and smuggling goods on a bus, and smoking the hours away in a shisha café. All these people were happy, unconcerned about achievements, or being historically significant. In fact, these contented souls accepted the circumstances of their birth, worked hard when needed, enjoyed what pleasures were available, and did not fret over when their next lucky break would come.

Travel had also taught me how much would happen entirely due to chance. There was no way to know when the clouds would roll in, the next person who would become my friend, or the next wrong turn that would lead to new opportunities. At the same time, backpacking had shown me that, no matter what happened, I would be able to muddle through. Just like every other human being on the planet.

My backpacking days did not bring any epiphany on what to do with my life. There was no answer, no perfect solution waiting to be found. I still did not know the color of my parachute. But it was a simple matter of taking a first step, and then seeing what happened. And then I would take the next step, just as I had been doing for the past eleven months.

It was time to begin my next adventure. I boarded a plane to Toronto, which would be my home for now.

Well ... at least that was the plan.

ACKNOWLEDGEMENTS

THIS STORY would never have been published except for the enthusiastic urging of Kara Samson. I am grateful for the encouragement and feedback from Carson Ling, Susie Nygard, Mark and Marnie Robson, and Fenton Fong. And of course, thank you to my wife Catherine for her patience and support.

Carl B. Yong lives in North Vancouver, Canada, with his wife and teenage son. His daughter attends the University of Victoria.

Printed in Canada